THE TRANSPARENT SELF

Revised Edition

SIDNEY M. JOURARD

THE TRANSPARENT SELF

D. VAN NOSTRAND COMPANY
NEW YORK / CINCINNATI / TORONTO / LONDON / MELBOURNE

D. Van Nostrand Company Regional Offices:
New York   Cincinnati
D. Van Nostrand Company International Offices:
London   Toronto   Melbourne

Copyright © 1971 by Litton Educational Publishing, Inc.

Library of Congress Catalog Card Number 72–147389

15   14   13   12

Preface to Second Edition

For nearly two centuries, the image of the melting pot served as a symbol of the United States. Newcomers were welcomed to this land of opportunity, but their heritage was melted away in the fires of the socialization process, to produce *homo Americanensis*. The "American" conquered the wildness, decimated the Indians, and is now in speedy course toward devastating natural resources, and the perspectives of other nations. It is time to replace the image of the melting pot with another metaphor—perhaps *mosaic* is apt. It is time for melting-pot America to become mosaic America, where myriad perspectives and ways to live are welcomed as part of the human drama, not suppressed as "unpatriotic."

If America and, indeed, the Western world, become "pluralistic" societies, then they will indeed be places suitable for "transparent selves." I dedicate this new edition of *The Transparent Self* to the passionate and, I hope, unbloody quest for social structures in which all who are of goodwill can live in harmony and mutual confirmation.

I have eliminated several chapters of the first edition from this revision because they seemed redundant. In their place, I added several which represent extensions of ideas first developed in the original edition, but which appear to fit with the overall aims of the book.

I want to thank Anne Morgan Nunez and Anne Taylor, both former students of mine and readers of the first edition, for helping me cut awkward phrasing wherever they found it. I did not follow their suggestions in all cases.

Sidney M. Jourard

Gainesville, Florida
1971

Preface to First Edition

A choice that confronts every one at every moment is this: Shall we permit our fellows to know us as we now are, or shall we remain enigmas, wishing to be seen as persons we are not?

This choice has always been available, but throughout history we have chosen to conceal our authentic being behind masks. We assume the *other* man is hiding or misrepresenting his real feelings, his intentions, or his past because we generally do so ourselves. We take it for granted that when a man speaks about himself, he is telling more or less than the unvarnished truth.

We camouflage our true being before others to protect our-selves against criticism or rejection. This protection comes at a steep price. When we are not truly known by the other people in our lives, we are misunderstood. When we are misunderstood, especially by family and friends, we join the "lonely crowd."*[99] Worse, when we succeed in hiding our being from others, we tend to lose touch with our real selves. This loss of self contributes to illness in its myriad forms.

It is curious that we psychologists have not seriously questioned man's *decision* to hide rather than to reveal himself. Indeed, self-concealment is regarded as the most natural state for grown men. People who reveal themselves in simple honesty are seen as childish or crazy, as was Billy Budd, in Melville's novel, or Prince Mishkin in Dostoyevsky's *The Idiot.* The assumption that concealment is a more natural state for man than candor has given rise to many stratagems for getting inside a man's defenses. These run the gamut from attempting to get a man drunk, to asking him to report his dreams or to tell what he sees in some inkblots. Here, the assumption is that he will then, in spite of himself, give hints of what he has been hiding.

Yet, our research shows that such methods of getting a person to "open up" are unnecessary when he *wants* to be known. At such times he will do everything in his power to make sure the other person's image of him is accurate. He will show the same concern to be known that a less honest person will to ensure the other has a false picture of him.

I became fascinated with self-disclosure after puzzling about the fact that patients who consulted me for therapy told me more about themselves than they had ever told another living person. Many of them said, "You are the first person I have ever been completely honest with." I wondered whether there was some connection between their reluctance to be known by spouse, family, and friends and their need to consult with a professional psychotherapist. My fascination with self-disclosure led to a conceptual and empirical odyssey, some aspects of which are described in the chapters that follow.

Another phenomenon, not completely separable from self-dis-

*The superscript numbers throughout the text refer to the numbered references in the bibliography.

closure, is *spirit*. There is increasing scientific evidence that man's physical and psychological health are profoundly affected by the degree to which he has found meaning, direction, and purpose in his existence. Some of this purpose and meaning arises in man's relationships with his fellows. I suspect a man's life begins to lose meaning most rapidly when he becomes estranged from his fellows; when he distrusts others so much he misleads them into thinking they know him when, in fact, he knows that they do not and cannot. "Spirit" is a term which scientists view with suspicion as a matter which does not lend itself to scientific study. Yet there is more to man than the structures and drives he shares with animals. Consequently, I have taken a fresh look at whatever there is that can be seen when the layman or poet speaks of spirit, and I have attempted to bring these phenomena within the scope of scientific analysis. Part of this book shows the result of my thinking in this area.

The book as a whole explores the hypothesis that man can attain to health and fullest personal development only insofar as he gains courage to be himself with others and when he finds goals that have meaning for him—including the reshaping of society so it is fit for all to live and grow in. I would like this book to be read by research psychologists, counselors and psychotherapists, ministers, nurses, and health scientists, as well as by students of mental health. And, of course, I welcome the attention of interested laymen who wish to become acquainted with recent thinking in a field that touches upon their potential for fuller functioning as human beings.

Sidney M. Jourard

Gainesville, Florida
1964

Acknowledgments

Parts of this book have appeared in the following journals: *Voices: The Art and Science of Psychotherapy* (Chapters 2 and 18); *Mental Hygiene* (Chapter 3); *Journal of Existential Psychiatry* (Chapters 4 and 10); *Journal of Humanistic Psychology* (Chapter 5); *Law and Contemporary Problems* (Chapter 8); *Journal of Individual Psychology* (Chapter 16); *American Journal of Nursing* (Chapters 20, 21, and 22). These articles are reproduced here with permission from the respective editors.

Chapter 11 appeared first in E. Shneideman (ed.), *On the Nature of Suicide* (San Francisco: Jossey-Bass, 1969). Chapter 12 was first published as a chapter in H. A. Otto (ed.), *The Family in Search of a Future* (New York: Appleton-Century-Crofts,

1970). Chapter 19 will also be published in L. Blank, M. Gottsegen, and Gloria Gottsegen (eds.), *Confrontation: Encounters in Self and Interpersonal Awareness* (New York: Collier-Macmillan, 1971). These chapters are reproduced here with the permission of the publishers.

Contents

PART THREE: INSPIRITATION AND WELLNESS

PART FOUR: TOWARD A SOCIETY FIT FOR HUMAN BEINGS

PART FIVE: THE DISCLOSING PSYCHOTHERAPIST

PART SIX: A HUMAN WAY OF BEING FOR NURSES (AND OTHER HELPING PROFESSIONALS)

A TECHNICAL APPENDIX FOR PSYCHOLOGISTS

PART 1

INTRODUCTION

1

Self-Disclosure and the Mysterious Other

I see my fellow man doing all manner of things, and I have no way of predicting or understanding why he does what he does. In fact, I may fear him, as I fear anything which acts with caprice. I may impute motives like mine to him, as primitive man imputed human motives to animals, the sea, plants, and the weather. I may engage in magic or ritual, as primitive men did, to get others to help me or leave me alone.

When man learned the conditions which were responsible for the behavior of the weather, the sea, plants, and animals, he feared them less and became more able to enlist their collaboration for the pursuit of his ends. He no longer imputed characteristics to these things which they did not possess, but strove, rather, to ascertain their real characteristics and to understand the forces which moved them. Man's fear changed then to respect.

With his fellow, however, man continues to behave as he did in earlier times with plants, animals, and elements. His beliefs about the other man are usually based on insufficient evidence, and they are thus often false. Consequently, a man may find himself living fearfully in a world of strangers whose actions are not understood.

The other man is a mystery. He is opaque. We cannot know in advance what he will do. We do not know his past, and we do not know what is "going on inside him." We remain on guard when we are in his presence.

The other man behaves predictably some of the time in the ritual of living. He clothes himself, goes to work, tips his hat to ladies, utters polite conversation, and in short, seems "normal"— unless he is a foreigner, a psychotic, a "hippie," or a child. In the latter instances, we may admit we don't know what he is thinking, and even if he tells us, we may not understand because we don't know his language. Or, erroneously, we may assume that we know his motives, thoughts, and reactions.

Even if "normal" people tell us what they are thinking, what they feel, believe, or daydream about, many of us feel we are being "snowed"—the man isn't leveling with us. Often, he is doing just that. We are shocked when we read that Mr. Jones, without warning, took a hatchet and butchered his family, whom he seemed to love so well.

> *Things are seldom what they seem,*
> *Skim milk masquerades as cream.*
> *Externals don't portray insides,*
> *Jekylls may be masking Hydes.*

Let me apologize for such atrocious verse and then point up a fact. Man, perhaps alone of all living forms, is capable of *being* one thing and *seeming* from his actions and talk to be something else. Not even animals and insects and fishes which Nature expertly camouflages can do this "seeming" at will; they do it by reflex.

If Mr. Jones had frankly disclosed his feelings and plans to you, then news of his butchery would have come as no surprise. You would have understood it. Perhaps you could have predicted it and interfered, thus saving the lives of his "loved ones."

When a man discloses his experience to another, fully, spontaneously, and honestly, then the mystery that he was decreases enormously. When a man discloses himself to me, my preconceptions about him are altered by the facts as they come forth— unless, of course, I have a vested interest in continuing to believe untruths about him.

In the general scheme of things, what consequences follow when men disclose their real selves, one to the other? Here are some of the obvious outcomes:

—They learn the extent to which they are similar, one to the other, and the extent to which they differ from one another in thoughts, feelings, hopes, reactions to the past, etc.

—They learn of the other man's needs, enabling them to help him or to ensure that his needs will not be met.

—They learn the extent to which this man accords with or deviates from moral and ethical standards.

Why do we disclose ourselves, and why do we not? Answers to this question are of enormous importance, since mutual ignorance seems to be at the root of all problems between family members or between citizens of different nations.

Researches I have conducted[51, 57] show that a person will permit himself to be known when he believes his audience is a man of goodwill. Self-disclosure follows an attitude of love and trust. If I love someone, not only do I strive to know him; I *also display my love by letting him know me.* At the same time, by so doing, I permit him to love me.

Loving is scary, because when you permit yourself to be known, you expose yourself not only to a lover's balm, but also to a hater's bombs! When he knows you, he knows just where to plant them for maximum effect.

In a poker game, no man discloses the content of his hand to the other players. Instead, he tries to dissemble. If he holds four aces, he tries to get the others to believe his hand is empty until it is time for the showdown. If he holds nothing, he pretends he has four aces, so he can get something for nothing. In a society which pits man against man, as in a poker game, people do keep a poker face; they wear a mask and let no one know what they are up to. In a society where man is for man, then the psychological iron curtain is dropped.

Our research, however, reveals a paradox. One expects people to be transparent within the family, but we find much evidence of dissembling, of lack of mutual disclosure. Children do not know their parents; fathers do not know what their children think, or what they are doing. Husbands and wives often are strangers one to the other to an incredible degree.

We are said to be a society dedicated to the pursuit of truth. Yet, disclosure of the truth, the truth of one's being, is often penalized. Impossible concepts of how man ought to be—which are often handed down from the pulpit—make man so ashamed of his true being that he feels obliged to seem different, if for no other reason than to protect his job. Yet, when a man does not acknowledge to himself who, what, and how he is, he is out of touch with reality, and he will sicken. No one can help him without access to the facts. And it seems to be another fact that no man can come to know himself except as an outcome of disclosing himself to another person. This is the lesson we have learned in the field of psychotherapy. When a person has been able to disclose himself utterly to another person, he learns how to increase his contact with his real self, and he may then be better able to direct his destiny on the basis of this knowledge.

Self-disclosure between men reduces the mystery that one man is for another. It is the empirical index of an I-Thou relationship, which I, agreeing with Buber,[10, 11] see as the index of man functioning at his highest and truly human level rather than at the level of a thing or an animal.

Self-disclosure, however, requires courage. Not solely the courage to be, as Paul Tillich[126] wrote of it, but the courage to be known, to be perceived by others as one knows himself to be. We can paraphrase the Delphic oracle who advised, "Know thyself," and declare, "Make thyself known, and thou shalt then know thyself." Finally, we can restate Polonius' advice to his son, ". . . And this above all—to any other man be true, and thou canst not then be false to thyself."

2

The Beginnings of
Self-Disclosure: A
Personal Narrative*

I shall discuss the way the scientific study ot self-disclosure came
into being, and where it has led. In telling the story, I will do a
certain amount of self-disclosure.

I have been a professional psychologist tor twenty years. As an
undergraduate, I was exposed to many of the same ideas, techniques, and theories that any contemporary "psych major" is exposed to. I was frustrated and bored with much of the psychology
I studied in undergraduate school at Toronto, with the dead and
deadly ideas and books that I was obliged to read and master. I
read and mastered them and remained a student of psychology.

*First presented as a talk at Florida Presbyterian College, St. Petersburg,
Florida, in November, 1969.

I was convinced that the study of man should be exciting and that it would throw some light on the human condition, on persons, and on my condition, because I, after all, was a human and a person!

I got little for me from the various textbooks on learning and motivation, the history of psychology, and so on. These texts seemed like third-rate biology and second-rate philosophy to me, and I was taking first-rate biology and philosophy in other courses. But I stuck to it and managed to survive undergraduate school. Graduate school was more exciting, because I was learning something about Freud, who was taboo at Toronto. In Buffalo he was less taboo. And I was learning how one person might become more adept at helping another person live his life. This is called counseling and psychotherapy. I was involved in receiving counseling and psychotherapeutic help, as part of my training as well as for personal reasons. I found psychology becoming more interesting but I still didn't quite fit. I always felt like an outsider, even in graduate school. I finally graduated and went to Emory University for my first job. Emory is a church-related school. The Emory ambiance, I found, was not so much congenial to life as to a certain cosmetic, genteel way of life called "being an Emory citizen." During my five years there, several exemplary Emory citizens in their forties died, perhaps a consequence of their way of life. I may have gotten the idea for dispiritation and the sickening implications of certain roles at that time. (See Part Three.)

I wasn't interested in studying the kinds of things my colleagues were investigating. With fear, trembling, and trepidation, I began studying things that interested me! And what interested me were problems that I was having trouble with in my life. At Buffalo, influenced by the psychoanalytic spirit, I became personally interested in ego strength. I wondered, "Do I have a strong ego?" "What does it mean to have a strong ego?" So I did my doctoral dissertation on ego strength.[52]

I had always been interested in bodies—in your body and mine, in how one felt about his body. So rather than doing studies of rat behavior, which didn't turn me on much, I worked out some simple techniques for measuring peoples' attitudes towards their own bodies. A colleague, Paul Secord, and I[65] cooperated in a number of studies of correlates of the way a person feels about his body and why he likes or dislikes different body parts.

One of the things I found rampant at Emory was what I called moral indignation. The faculty, especially faculty wives, were very ready to gossip and backbite about any kind of behavior that to them seemed deviant. I found this problematic, so I did a study in moral indignation.[54] One of the things I noticed was that, though our neighbors on "faculty row" would gossip viciously about offbeat characters, they would never ever criticize their mamas and their papas. So I thought, "Good heavens, is there a correlation between moral indignation and repression of anger and hostility toward one's parents?" I developed a technique for measuring attitude towards one's parents and another technique for measuring moral indignation. I tested a lot of people with these instruments and found a low, but significant correlation. The more morally indignant the people were toward offbeat behavior, the less they criticized their parents and the more they glorified them.

When I left Emory, as inevitably I had to (I didn't have to, as a matter of fact; I was just told, "You can stay here as long as you like, but there's no future for you here."), I took a job in a psychiatry department at double the salary. During that time, I became fascinated with self-disclosure.

While at Emory, I wrote a textbook. The galleys of this book were available when I moved to the University of Alabama's Psychiatry Department in Birmingham. I was reading my own material and finding it fascinating. Somewhere,[55] in what I had written, I discussed the "real self" and what it means to be a "real self," and I wrote of the connection between "real-self being" and healthy personality. The whole idea of being a self, and being a real self I'd gotten out of reading Karen Horney.[40, 45] Through Karen Horney, I was introduced to Kierkegaarde.

As a scientist, I wondered, "How do you measure real-self being?" This scientific question was connected with an existential question with which I had been wrestling just about all of my life:

"Am I a liar, a fraud and a phony? Or am I for real?" Following the trend of my career, I tried to study this question experimentally. I'm leading up to how it came to pass that I developed a technique for measuring self-disclosure. It is a tortuous path, but journal articles never tell you this sort of thing. In any journal article, the author says, "The following hypothesis was proposed, this method was devised, these were the subjects, these were the techniques, and these were the results." It doesn't work like that at all. When you are a researcher, you grope, bungle, and fumble.

I was unhappy in the psychiatry department. I had a showdown with my boss, who invited me to change my ways. If I would do so, I could stay there forever. If I chose to continue being a psychologist in the way I thought was meaningful, he let me know I could leave. I opted to leave. I started applying for other jobs. My prospective employers sent all kinds of questionnaires sometimes asking very personal questions. I filled out answers thinking the while, "I'm giving these employers a view of me that in some cases is more detailed than my friends and family have." And I thought, "Who else knows the things about myself that I'm telling an employer?"

Then I got excited. I saw the possibility of a measuring device. If you're a researcher, you can't do much research unless you can measure something or other. So I went around asking my friends and colleagues, "What do you know about me?" I would listen to them tell me what they thought they knew about me, and I hardly recognized myself. Then I reciprocated and told them what I thought I knew about them on the basis of what they had told me.

In a certain sense, every person is an animated questionnaire. Each of us embodies a whole batch of questions that we address to everyone whom we contact. As they behave before us and tell us about themselves, mentally we tick off answers to such questions as "Is he honest? Is he Protestant? Does he go to college? Is he married?" In fact, some people have only one or two questions about others, while more complex people carry many questions. One doesn't always make these questions explicit, but as a person presents himself to you, he is answering questions of yours, thus reducing uncertainty about people in general and that person in particular. And all I was doing was making this existential practice explicit.

With a bit of fiddling, I was able to arrive at a list of questions that people ask of one another when their aim is to come to know one another personally. I came to call this list a Self Disclosure Questionnaire.* I was excited with it, and I tested everybody I could. A sociologist colleague, the late Paul Lasakow, helped me in the first projects. We asked people to indicate on the questionnaire which categories of information they had revealed to certain other people. The questions were of this sort: "What are your food likes and dislikes?" "What are your personal religious views?" "How do you feel about your own body?" I wasn't asking them to tell me this information. I was asking them to indicate the topics they had disclosed to their mother, their father, their closest friend of the same sex, and their closest friend of the opposite sex, or their spouse. I was hoping to get a broad survey of the degree to which certain classes of people had disclosed themselves. This led to a series of studies we published over a six- or seven year period. [49-51, 56-64] We reported that women have disclosed more personal data about themselves to the significant people in their lives than men. Whites have disclosed more than comparable blacks to significant people in their lives. American college students have disclosed more about themselves to their parents and peers than have college students tested in England, Puerto Rico, the Near East, and Germany. It appears that Americans, by contrast with other nationalities, are more verbally self-revealing. (See pages 225 to 233.)

By 1958 I was working in a nursing college. There, we found that nursing students who showed themselves to be the most disclosing to their parents and their peers turned out to be much better at establishing close communicative relations with patients when they got on to clinical work than low-disclosing students. Moreover, they got better grades in nursing college.[58] There

*See Appendices 1 and 2.

seemed to be some kind of connection between readiness to be open and disclosing to people in one's personal life and the ability to establish a warm, communicative helping relationship in this professional situation.* I could multiply these examples, but a book will be published soon that summarizes all our research in self-disclosure.[57] I will just give some highlights.

One thing we found in our questionnaire studies fascinated me; we found a correlation between what persons were willing to disclose to other people in their life and what these other people had disclosed to them.[59, 62, 64] There appeared to be a reciprocity in self-disclosure. The questionnaire findings fascinated me, because at that time I was going through a crisis in my ways of being a professional counselor and psychotherapist. I was quite well trained in two main schools of psychotherapeutic theory and technique: the client-centered approach of Carl Rogers and a modified psychoanalytic approach. Neither of these ways of being a psychotherapist, of trying to help a person live his life more effectively, worked for me. In fact, when I was faced by someone who behaved toward me like a client-centered counselor or a psychoanalyst, it would almost make me vomit because it seemed inauthentic.

I was never in therapy with a "Rogerian,"** but one of my colleagues lived this approach. She and I did part-time vocational counseling for the VA. One day I went to work feeling terribly depressed. I said to my then colleague, "Oh, Gloria, I don't know if I can face today. I feel rotten." Gloria, a Ph.D., turned to me. Up to that point, it had been "Sid," and "Gloria." But as soon as I uttered my despair and depression, a glaze came over her eyes. I felt myself transmuted from "Sid" into a "client." Her face assumed an expression that was supposed to be warmth, and she said, "You feel pretty rotten, don't you Sid." That ended the dialogue as far as I was concerned. That happened at Buffalo while I was finishing my doctoral training.

*The experience of working in the College of Nursing culminated in the papers in Part Six of this book.
**Carl Rogers, himself, is no "Rogerian."

When I was at Emory, I had to do psychotherapeutic work to supplement my inadequate salary. I started a part-time private practice, and the ways of being a psychotherapist in which I had been trained simply did not work! They worked fine in Buffalo with middle class, urban, intellectual college students and college graduates; however, they did not work with provincial people, one decade away from a farm or a small town. I had to learn to be effective as a therapist with these people because my training seemed irrelevant. Through trial and error I found that if I abandoned my psychotherapeutic techniques and presented myself as a fairly intelligent, well-intentioned human being, if I shared some of my experience with problems similar to the ones that my patients were wrestling with, we got a good working relationship going. This was quite a departure from the orthodox techniques in which I had been trained, and I felt anxious about it. But my research in self-disclosure was showing that disclosure invites or begets disclosure. My changes in psychotherapeutic behavior confirmed this. There's no way to force somebody to talk about himself. You can only invite. The most powerful and relevant invitation I could find was to share my subjectivity with the other. The research and my applied work interpenetrated and influenced each other.* I continued with various forms of research in self-disclosure but I began to question the very field of applied psychology.

When someone is a psychiatrist, a clinical psychologist, or social worker, or, for that matter, a pastoral counselor, and he seeks to help people, the question immediately has to be raised, "Help them do or be what?" A psychiatrist doesn't have any trouble. He says, "I'm trying to cure a person of his mental disease." And a psychologist might say, "I'm trying to correct some maladaptive behavior." It doesn't matter what rhetoric or idiom you use, the counselor sees himself as a professional helper; he's involved in one of the "helping professions." But I began to wonder if professional helpers were not so much helping people discover their

*The chapters in Part Five of this book and those on psychotherapy in my 1968 book[50] grew from this experience.

own possibilities and live them as they were unwittingly helping people to confine themselves to a way of being that maintained a social or family status quo. If that happened to be true, then you could view sick or maladjusted people as unenlightened and ineffective revolutionaries and the professional helper as an agent of social control, that is, as some kind of counter-revolutionary. That didn't appeal to me very much. I did not like to see myself as a counter-revolutionary agent for the status quo.

There appeared to be two possible ways for a psychotherapist to relate to the social system. This fascinated me. I could see that a professional counselor or psychotherapist is a professional inviter of self-disclosure. The implicit promise is that if a patient discloses his sins and peccadillos, he will benefit from it beyond the sheer emotional "catharsis." But the helpful suggestions and interpretations of the therapist may function as a kind of social control.

Now I could see, as the late Frank Shaw said,[114] that a professional counselor could function as a kind of enlightener, as a guide to more enlightened and liberated existence for the person consulting with him. This perspective lifted counseling and psychotherapy outside the manipulative, medical model. Patients could be seen as unenlightened seekers, trying to find a guru, a person who would help them find their authentic path. This raised another question. "Who, then, functions as a guru?" Not someone who is the master of a bunch of technical tricks, but someone who by his very way of living and being excites admiration and attracts followers. Then I would look at myself and my colleagues, and say, "Good God, who would want to follow us, anyway? In the first place, we don't let our clients know us as we really are; we regard that as nonprofessional conduct. If you look at us, you see many of us are fat, lifeless, constipated, victims of the occupational diseases that come from a sedentary life." I began to suggest at professional meetings, workshops, and conventions that professional counselors should let the client interview them as thoroughly as they intend to interview the client. I wasn't able to encourage many of my colleagues to follow that way. But I was finding that when I let my clients come to know me within the context of an ongoing dialogue, then I got to know them; and that elusive phenomenon called trust would be generated on a much more sensible basis. I found that the outcomes of our counseling or therapeutic transactions were much more mutually satisfying. Moreover, I didn't have the feeling I was functioning as an unwitting agent of social control.

My research in self-disclosure, part of the quest for knowledge for its own sake, had implications for my work as a clinician. In that capacity I was concerned with defining "mental health" and ways to foster it. If authentic self-disclosure was a factor in mental health and if disclosure begets disclosure, then it made sense for a therapist to be an exemplar of the way he was inviting his client to follow, if the client was to be liberated from his headaches, impotence, and other consequences of inauthenticity.

Then I hit upon another idea. I don't know how it came to me. I think I thought of it as I read over some of my own articles. It had to do with the very foundation of every kind of behavioral science: namely, the human relationship that is established between the scientific investigator and the human being whom he is studying.

Man has to be willing to show himself. There are sneaky surveillance techniques that one can employ to spy on others.* Some colleagues published a book entitled *Unobtrusive Measures*[129] which describes techniques worthy of the CIA. The CIA and private detectives, however, are more diabolically skillful at getting and recording your self-disclosure—even when you seek to be unobserved. The TV program, "Mission Impossible," and "Dick Tracy" both show sneaky means by which someone can pick up your verbal and behavioral disclosures. Everybody leaves traces on the sands and ether of time. To leave tracks is to disclose something about yourself. Now, unwitting disclosure is different from willful disclosure. In the latter instance your aim is to let another person know with no shadow of a doubt what you have

*Hence, Chapter 8 of the present volume, concerned with man's need for privacy

done, what you feel, etc. Unwitting disclosure is disclosure of what you don't want people to know—in fact, you might rather die than let them know. Man is singular under the sun in that, better than any other living species, he can lie and dissemble. No other being can lie, dissemble, and mimic in as many dimensions as man can. A chameleon can mimic the color of his surroundings. A live possum can imitate a dead possum. Mockingbirds and parrots can mimic the sounds of other birds. But man is the master of the mendacious arts. If this is true and if students of human experience and behavior are interested in learning something about man, then *the relationship between the person being studied and the one studying him is called into question.* If you want to study me and I don't know you or trust you, I'll kick you out, or I'll lie to you.

We learned something in our researches about the conditions under which people are willing to make dimensions of themselves known to others. One of these conditions was *mutual* disclosure. Partners in dialogue let one another know one another apace. This seemed to be true in effective counseling and psychotherapy. It appears to be true in meaningful marriages and friendships. The questions that began to obsess me were: "To what extent do the subjects of psychological research know and trust the researchers who study them, analyze the findings, develop theories, and then write learned articles and books? To what extent are the experimenters trustworthy?" Lots of subjects in psychological research have discovered that the researcher has lied to them in order to test some hypothesis. Psychologists have gotten the reputation of being notorious tricksters and liars. If subjects didn't trust them, it shouldn't be too much of a shock or surprise. Then, too, psychologists are human like everybody else. Some of us work for advertising firms, manufacturers, the military, and other concerns where the aim in studying man is not to help the man who is being studied, but to help the person who is paying for the research costs. It is not grossly unfair to say that some psychologists and sociologists are literally government agents. Nor is it unfair from this perspective to say they could be regarded as spies. If that is true (and incidentally, this is in no way to impugn the scientific integrity of any of my colleagues), it wouldn't be too surprising if many subjects of psychological research misrepresented their experience and their behavior before the recording apparatus of the behavioral scientist. That raised the fascinating, and at the same time horrible, possibility (not so horrible, because it's not so surprising) that eighty years of scientific research in psychology, as it reposes on the library shelves, may not embody an authentic image of man. In fact, it may be a museum of the lies told by suspicious subjects to experimenters they did not trust. I therefore proposed that we do all of psychology over again.

I was excited with this idea, and I shared it from lecture platforms at conventions in London, Aberdeen, Oslo, Washington, New York City, and Ottawa, to mention a few places. I would present my view of the research situation and then invite my colleagues to start doing all psychology over again. They declined, and said, "Why don't you do it?" I said, "All right, I can't do all of it, but I'll start." So we started.

One of the advantages of being a professor is that you have graduate students. So, with the help of graduate students, we have begun the task. In five years, we have done only a tiny amount on this immodest project. How have we gone about it? We have done various studies in the way in which they were done originally, or in a way they would traditionally be done. Under such conditions, the experimenter presents himself as Mr. or Dr. So-and-so. He asks the subject to fill out forms or respond to some equipment, and the experiment is run. Then we do it over again with another group of subjects. Before the experiment is carried out, the researcher and each person get acquainted as persons through reciprocal dialogue. The subject comes to know who the researcher is and what he's up to. If the researcher is reluctant to tell what his hypotheses are, he can say, "Well I don't want to tell you what we're looking for." But this statement is made in the context of mutual disclosure so that the subject doesn't feel that a trick is being played on him. In short, the researcher makes an effort to let the subject know him. These experiments, done the same way as traditional experiments but with this important difference, produce different outcomes, as you might expect.[51]

That seems exciting to me, and it promises to yield a more complete image of man. We seem to be following Egon Brunswick's suggestion to do research growing out of "representative design," in which you study the behavior of the person in a representative sample of his existential situations.

In the midst of this work in self-disclosure, I became interested in a branch of philosophic endeavor called "existential phenomenology."* This refers to the study of experience, or consciousness, as it is lived by each individual. I read works of Husserl, Heidegger, Sartre, Buber, and Merleau-Ponty. I spent the year 1964–65 studying with Ronald Laing in London. He is a psychiatrist and a gifted existential phenomenologist to boot. This line of philosophic thought was very relevant to my concern with self-disclosure. One of the exciting things I found in reading this literature was the very term "disclosure." To disclose means to unveil, to make manifest, or to show. *Self*-disclosure is the act of making yourself manifest, showing yourself so others can perceive you.

Everything and everybody in the world disclose themselves by one means or another as long as they exist. All of a sudden it makes sense for me to say that a tree discloses its "treeness." "To receive the disclosure of the world" becomes another way of defining the term "perception." To perceive is to receive the disclosure of something. And so I became fascinated with the question "What disclosure of the world do I *receive*?" Never mind what disclosure I give to the world, deliberate and unintentional, but how much of the disclosure of the world do I receive?

As soon as you ask this question of yourself or of another person, it appears that some people, bombarded as we all are by the disclosure of the world, receive nothing. It is as if they are blind, deaf, and anosmic. Some other people are more receptive to the disclosure of the world. Here is a fresh, new definition of

*Chapters 11, 13, 14, 18, and 19 reflect this influence.

what education is supposed to do: to open the doors of perception, as Blake put it, to help a person receive and make sense of more of the disclosure of the world. We then can understand one of the reasons why people dive into marijuana and psychedelic drugs to have the experience of receiving more of the world's disclosure. We can also understand what the hippies call "freaking somebody out" in the light of this analysis. A hippie may, with a certain amount of mischief and malice, talk to or simply show his hirsute appearance to a very "square" person. The very "square" person will become irrationally angry because something has just come into his world which isn't the way it ought to be. One then begins to think of Kurt Goldstein's[36] patients of World War I, when he did the classical studies of concrete behavior in brain-damaged people. These patients had gunshot wounds to the head that produced various degrees of brain damage. Goldstein noted that they had lost the ability to assume the "abstract attitude," and, more importantly, they displayed a "catastrophic reaction" to any introduction of change into their world. That is, following the head injury, as long as their world was kept fanatically tidy and stable, they could function well; but put their shoes to the left instead of the right of the bed or present them with some new task for which they had not been prepared, and they might faint, go into a near homicidal rage, or go into tremendous panic.

Many people "educated" in our public school system, react to new ideas with outrage or panic as Goldstein's patients did. Can we regard public education as a functional equivalent to a gunshot wound to the head? Do our socialization practices have effects comparable to brain tumors and arteriosclerosis?

I started this discussion and the research that it grew out of around this question: "Under what conditions will you and I make our mysterious subjectivity available to the perception of others?" That is what self-disclosure is about. I wind up with the reverse of this question: "Under what conditions am I able to receive and make sense out of the unremitting disclosure of the world?" In the process of wrestling with these questions, it became possible to take a fresh look at education, psychotherapy, psychedelic drugs, brain damage, and even the mass media. To what extent, for example, do radio, television, the movies, and newspapers open you to more of the disclosure of the world so that you can make unique sense out of it, and to what extent do they blind you or try to influence the way in which you attach meaning to the disclosure of the world you receive? Disclosure is a fascinating business.

PART 2

Self-Disclosure and
Human Existence

3

Healthy Personality
and Self-Disclosure

For a long time, health and well-being have been taken for granted as "givens," and disease has been viewed as the problem for man to solve. Today, however, increasing numbers of scientists have begun to adopt a reverse point of view; disease and trouble are the givens, and specification of positive health and its conditions are viewed as the important goal. Physical, mental, and social health are values representing restrictions on the total variance of being. The scientific problem here consists in defining health, determining its relevant dimensions, and identifying the independent variables of which these are a function.[55, 80]

Scientists, however, are supposed to be hard-boiled, and they insist that phenomena in order to be counted "real" must be public. Hence, many behavioral scientists ignore man's "self"—his experience of his situation—since it is essentially a private phenomenon. Others, however, are not so quick to allocate man's self to the limbo of the unimportant, and they insist that we cannot understand man and his lot until we take his experience into account.

I fall into the camp of those investigators who want to explore health as a positive problem in its own right and who, further, take man's self seriously—as a reality to be explained and as a variable which produces consequences for weal or woe. In this chapter, I would like more fully to explore the connection between positive health and the disclosure of self. First, some sociological truisms.

Social systems require their members to take certain roles. Unless the roles are adequately fulfilled, the social systems will not produce the results for which they have been organized. This applies to systems as simple as one developed by an engaged couple and to those as complex as a total nation among nations.

Societies have socialization "factories" and "mills"—families and schools—which serve the function of training people to take on the age, sex, and occupational roles which they shall be obliged to fulfill throughout their life in the social system.[90] Broadly speaking, if a person carries out his roles suitably, he can be regarded as a "normal" personality. *Normal personalities, however, are not necessarily healthy personalities.*[55]

Man has more to do with his energies than use them merely to produce popularity, approval, or mediocre anonymity in the mass. Yet many people seek these outcomes to action as ends in themselves, as the *summum bonum* to which all other considerations are subordinated. The curious thing is that, if a man places normality at the pinnacle of importance, many other values are in fact jeopardized. It is a matter of indifference to the social system whether such conformity is achieved at the price of idiosyncratic need gratifications, a sense of identity and selfhood, creativity, or even physical health. Such official indifference to all a man's being save his role conformity has longer-run deleterious effects on the social system. It costs the system progress and innovation. It makes for a "closed" and stagnant society rather than one which is "open."[92]

It is a truth that normality (role conformity) in some social systems produces physical illness of gradual onset; and if too many real idiosyncratic needs are stifled in the pursuit and maintenance of normality, then boredom, neurosis, or psychosis will be regular, predictable outcomes.

The "sociology of illness" tabulates incidents of assorted diseases in various age, sex, socioeconomic, and subcultural groupings—incidences which exceed those found in the population at large. For example, peptic ulcer occurs more commonly among men than among women, and schizophrenia occurs more commonly among lower-class people than among upper-middle-class folk. These correlations should not come as any surprise, for the illnesses arise for one reason, and one reason only: *the people who live the ways of life typical to their social position become ill because they behave in ways exquisitely calculated to produce just those outcomes.* They sicken because they behave in sickening ways.

TRANSPARENCY TO ONESELF

It should be true that healthy behavior feels "right," and it should produce growth and integrity of the system, "man." By "integrity" I mean resistance to illness, disintegration, or disorganization. Doubtless, when a person is behaving in ways that do violence to his integrity, warning signals are emitted. If only man could recognize these, diagnose them himself, and institute corrective action! Then he would live a hundred years. The potential of warning signals is capitalized upon by designers of machines; they build indicators which flash lights when output exceeds tolerances or when intakes are outside a specified range. Fuses blow, governors go into action, and power is shut off. "Normal" self-alienated man, however, often ignores his "tilt" signals—

anxiety, guilt, fatigue, boredom, pain, or frustration—and continues actions aimed at wealth, power, or normality until his body "shrieks" loudly enough to be heard. The meaning of sickness is *protest*; it is the protest of a system which has sent warning signals to the "communication center" only to have these ignored. If ignored long enough, the system will no longer mediate even normal behavior, much less optimum behavior. Sickness saves the remnant of the system from total destruction by preventing further operation, until "needs"—inputs—are taken care of. In fact, "being sick"—going to bed—is behavior undertaken to restore integrity. It is often the only behavior a person has available in our culture to secure some kinds of satisfactions which his "normal" mode of action fails to produce, e.g., passivity or authenticity. What a tragedy that in our society the only authentic "being" we are permitted by others and which we permit ourselves is being sick, and sometimes being drunk!

SELF-DISCLOSURE AND HEALTHY PERSONALITY

Healthy personalities play their roles satisfactorily and derive personal satisfaction from role enactment; more, they keep growing and they maintain high-level wellness.[21] It is probably enough, speaking from the standpoint of a stable social system, for people to be normal personalities. But it is possible to be a normal personality and be absolutely miserable. We would count such a normal personality unhealthy. In fact, normality in some social systems—successful acculturation to them—reliably produces ulcers, piles, paranoia, or compulsiveness. We also have to regard as unhealthy those people who have never been able to enact the roles that legitimately can be expected from them.

Counselors, guidance workers, and psychotherapists are obliged to treat both patterns of unhealthy personality—those people who have been unable to learn their roles and those who play their roles quite well, but suffer agonies of boredom, anxiety, or stultification. If our clients are to be helped, they must change in valued directions. A change in a valued direction may be called growth. We who are professionally concerned with the happiness and growth of our clients may be regarded as professional lovers, not unlike the Cyprian sisterhood. It would be fascinating to pursue this parallel further, but for the moment let us ask instead what this has to do with self-disclosure.

To answer this question, let's tune in on an imaginary interview between a client and his counselor. The client says, "I have never told this to a soul, doctor, but I can't stand my wife, my mother is a nag, my father is a bore, and my boss is an absolutely hateful and despicable tyrant. I have been carrying on an affair for the past ten years with the lady next door, and at the same time I am a deacon in the church." The counselor says, showing great understanding and empathy, "Mm-humm!"

If we listened long enough we would find the client talks and talks about himself to this highly sympathetic and empathic listener. Later, the client may say, "Gosh, you have helped me a lot. I see what I must do and I will go ahead and do it."

Self-disclosure is a factor in effective counseling or psychotherapy. Would it be too arbitrary to assume people come to need help because they have not disclosed themselves in some optimum degree to the people in their lives?

An historical digression: Toward the end of the 19th century, Joseph Breuer discovered (probably accidentally) that when his hysterical patients talked about themselves, disclosing not only the verbal content of their memories, but also the feelings that they had suppressed at the time of assorted "traumatic" experiences, their hysterical symptoms disappeared. Somewhere along the line, Breuer withdrew from a situation which would have made him Freud's peer in history's hall of fame. When Breuer permitted his patients "to be," it scared him, one gathers, because some of his female patients disclosed themselves to be quite sexy, and what was probably worse, they felt sexy toward him. Freud did not flinch. He made the momentous discovery that neurotic people of his time were struggling like mad to avoid "being," to avoid being known, and to avoid "becoming."[2] He learned that his patients, when they were given the opportunity to "be" (which free association on a couch is nicely designed to do), would disclose that they had all manner of horrendous thoughts and feelings which they did not even dare disclose to themselves, much less express in the presence of another person. Freud[31] learned to permit his patients to be, through permitting them to disclose themselves utterly to another human. He evidently did not trust anyone enough to be willing to disclose himself *vis-à-vis*, so he disclosed himself to himself on paper and learned the extent to which he was himself self-alienated. Roles for people in Victorian days were even more restrictive than today, and Freud discovered that when people struggled to avoid being and knowing themselves, they got sick. They could only become well and stay relatively well when they came to know themselves through self-disclosure to another person.

SICKENING ROLES

Let me distinguish here between role relationships and interpersonal relationships—a distinction often overlooked in the spate of literature that deals with human relations. Roles are inescapable. They must be played or else the social system will not work. A role is a repertoire of behavior patterns which must be rattled off in appropriate contexts, and all behavior irrelevant to the role must be suppressed. But what we often forget is the fact that it is a *person* who is playing the role. This person has a self, or I should say he *is* a self. All too often the roles that a person plays do not do justice to all of his self. In fact, there may be nowhere that he may just *be* himself. Even more, the person may not *know* his self. He may be self-alienated. His real self becomes a feared and distrusted stranger. Estrangement, alienation from one's real self, is at the root of the "neurotic personality of our time" so eloquently described by Horney.[44, 45] Fromm[34] referred to the same phenomenon as a "socially patterned defect." Self-alienation is a sickness so widely shared that no one recognizes it. We may take it for granted that all the clients whom we encounter are self-alienated to a greater or lesser extent. If you ask anyone to answer the question, "Who are you?" the answer will generally be "I am a psychologist," "a businessman," "a teacher," or what have you. The respondent will probably tell you the name of the role with which he feels most closely identified. As a matter of fact, the respondent spends a great part of his life trying to discover who he is, and once he has made some such discovery, he spends the rest of his life trying to play the part. Of course, some of the roles—age, sex, family, or occupational roles—may be so restrictive that they fit a person in a manner not too different from the girdle of a 200-pound lady who is struggling to look like Brigitte Bardot. There is Faustian drama all about us in this world of role playing. Everywhere we see people who have sold their souls (or their real selves) for roles: psychologist, businessman, nurse, physician, this or that.

It is possible to be involved in a social group such as a family or a work setting for years and years, playing one's roles nicely with the other members—and never getting to know the persons who are playing the other roles. Roles can be played personally and impersonally, as we are beginning to discover. A husband can be married to his wife for fifteen years and never come to know her. He knows her as "the wife." This is the loneliness which people try to counter with "togetherness."[99] But much of today's "togetherness" is like the "parallel play" of two-year-old children, or like the professors in Stringfellow Barr's[5] novel who lecture past one another alternately and sometimes simultaneously. There is no real self-to-self or person-to-person meeting in such transactions.

There is probably no experience more terrifying than disclosing oneself to "significant others" whose probable reactions are assumed, but not known. Hence the phenomenon of "resistance." This is what makes psychotherapy so difficult to take, and so difficult to administer. If there is any skill to be learned in the art of counseling and psychotherapy, it is the art of coping with the terrors which attend self-disclosure and the art of decoding the language, verbal and nonverbal, in which a person speaks about his inner experience.

Self-disclosure is a symptom of personality health and a means of ultimately achieving healthy personality. When I say that self-disclosure is a symptom of personality health, I mean a person who displays many of the other characteristics that betoken healthy personality *will also display the ability to make himself fully known to at least one other significant human being.* When I say that self-disclosure is a means by which one achieves personality health, I mean it is not until I am my real self and I act my real self that my real self is in a position to grow. One's self grows from the *consequence of being.* People's selves stop growing when they repress them. This growth-arrest in the self is what helps to account for the surprising paradox of finding an infant inside the skin of someone who is playing the role of an adult. Jurgen Ruesch[107] describes assorted neurotics, psychotics, and psychosomatic patients as persons with selective atrophy and overspecialization in various aspects of the process of communication. This culminates in a foul-up of the processes of knowing others and of becoming known to others. Neurotic and psychotic symptoms might be viewed as smoke screens interposed between the patient's real self and the gaze of the onlooker. We might call symptoms "devices to avoid becoming known."[13, 86]

Alienation from one's real self not only arrests personal growth; it tends to make a farce out of one's relationships with people. The crucial "break" in schizophrenia is with *sincerity*, not reality.[3]

NONDISCLOSURE, STRESS, AND SICKNESS

Selye[112] proposed the hypothesis that illness as we know it arises in consequence of stress. Now I think unhealthy personality has a similar root cause, one which is related to Selye's concept of stress. Every maladjusted person is a person who has not made himself known to another human being and in consequence does not know himself. Nor can he be himself. More than that, he *struggles actively to avoid becoming known by another human being.* He *works* at it ceaselessly, twenty-four hours daily, and it is work![19, 20] In the effort to avoid becoming known, a person provides for himself a cancerous kind of stress which is subtle and unrecognized, but none the less effective in producing not only the assorted patterns of unhealthy personality which psychiatry talks about, but also the wide array of physical ills that have come to be recognized as the province of psychosomatic medicine.[1]

Some Lethal Aspects
of the Male Role

Men die sooner than women. Health scientists and public health officials have become justly concerned about the sex difference in death age. Biology provides no convincing evidence to prove that female organisms are intrinsically more durable than male ones or that tissues or cells taken from males are less viable than those taken from females. A promising place to look for an explanation of the perplexing sex differential in mortality is in the transactions between men and their environments, especially their interpersonal environments. In principle, there must be ways of behaving among people which prolong a man's life and ensure his fuller functioning, and ways of behaving which speed a man's progress toward death. What aspects of being a man in American society are related to man's faster rate of dying?

The male role requires man to appear tough, objective, striving, achieving, unsentimental, and emotionally unexpressive.[90] But seeming is not being. If a man *is* tender (behind his *persona*), if he weeps, if he shows weakness, he will probably regard himself as inferior to other men.

Now, from all we can fathom about the *subjective* side of man, men are as capable as women of responding to the play of life's events with a broad range of feelings. Man's potential thoughts, feelings, wishes and fantasies know no bounds, save those set by his biological structure and his personal history. But the male role, and the male's self-structure will not allow man to acknowledge or to disclose the entire breadth and depth of his inner experience to himself or to others. Man seems obliged, rather, to hide much of his real self—the ongoing flow of his spontaneous inner experience—from himself and from others.

MANLINESS AND LOW SELF-DISCLOSURE

Research[49, 63, 64] has shown that men typically reveal less personal information about themselves to others than women. Since men, doubtless, have as much "self," i.e. inner experience, as women, then it follows that men have more secrets from the interpersonal world than women. It follows further that men, seeming to dread being known by others, must be more continually tense (neuromuscular tension) than women. It is as if being manly implies the necessity to wear the neuromuscular "armor" of which Reich[95] wrote with such lucidity. Moreover, if a man has something to hide, it must follow that other people will be a threat to him; they might pry into his secrets, or he may, in an unguarded moment, reveal his true self in its nakedness, thereby exposing his areas of weakness and vulnerability. Naturally, when a person is in hostile territory, he must be continually alert, tense, opaque, and restless. All this implies that trying to seem manly is a kind of work, and work imposes stress and consumes energy. Manliness, then, seems to carry with it a chronic burden of stress and energy expenditure which could be a factor related to man's relatively shorter life-span.

If self-disclosure is an empirical index of openness and if openness is a factor in health and wellness, then research in self-disclosure seems to point to one of the potentially lethal aspects of the male role. Men keep their selves to themselves and impose thereby an added burden of stress beyond that imposed by the exigencies of everyday life. The experience of psychosomatic physicians who undertake psychotherapy with male patients suffering peptic ulcers, essential hypertension, and kindred disorders seems to support this contention.[1] Psychotherapy is the art of promoting self-disclosure and authentic being in patients who withhold their real selves from expression, and clinical experience shows that, when psychotherapy has been effective with psychosomatic patients, the latter change their role-definitions, their self-structures, and their behavior in the direction of greater spontaneity and openness with salutory consequences to their bodies. The time is not far off when it will be possible to demonstrate with adequately controlled experiments the nature and degree of correlation between levels and amounts of self-disclosure and proneness to illness and/or an early death age.

MANLINESS: THE LACK OF INSIGHT AND EMPATHY

There is another implication of the fact that men are lower self-disclosers than women, an implication that relates to self-insight. Men, trained by their upbringing to assume the "instrumental role," tend more to relate to other people on an I—It[10] basis than women. They are more adept than women at relating impersonally to others, seeing them as the embodiment of their roles rather than as persons enacting roles. Studies of leadership show that the leaders of the most effective groups maintain an optimum "distance" from their followers, thereby avoiding the distraction of overly intimate personal knowledge of the followers' immediate feelings and needs.[26]

Women (often to the despair of businesslike men) seem to find it difficult to keep their interpersonal relationships *impersonal;* they sense and respond to the feelings of the other person even in a supposedly official transaction, and they respond to their own feelings[59] toward the other person, seeming to forget the original purpose of the impersonal transaction.

Now, one outcome of effective psychotherapy is that the patient becomes increasingly sensitized to the nuances of his own feelings (and those of the therapist) as they ebb and flow in the relationship. The patient becomes more transparent to himself! Coincident with this increase in insight is an increase in empathy with others, an increase in his ability to "imagine the real."[11]

Personal life calls for insight and empathy in men as well as in women. If practice at spontaneous self-disclosure promotes insight and empathy, then perhaps we have here one of the mechanisms by which women become more adept at these aspects of their "expressive" role. Women, trained toward motherhood and a comforting function, engage in and receive more self-disclosure than men.[64] They are more "transparent selves" than men.

Let us now focus upon "insight," in the sense that we have used the term here. If men are trained to ignore their own feelings in order more adequately to pursue the instrumental aspects of manliness, it follows that they will be less sensitive to "all is not well signals" as these arise in themselves. The hypothesis may be proposed that women, more sensitized to their inner experience, will notice their "all is not well signals" sooner and more often than men and change their mode of existence to one more conducive to wellness, e.g., consult a doctor sooner,* or seek bed rest more often than men. Men, by contrast, fail to notice these "all is not well signals" of weaker intensity and do not stop work or take to their beds until the destructive consequences of their

---

*I think a survey would show that more women than men consult physicians and psychotherapists.

manly way of life have progressed to the point of a "stroke" or a total collapse. It is as if women "amplify" such inner distress signals even when they are dim, while men, as it were, "tune them out" until they become so strong they can no longer be ignored.[32]

Accordingly, manly men, unaccustomed to self-disclosure and characterized by lesser insight and lesser empathy than women, do violence to their own unique needs and persist in modes of behavior which, to be sure, are effective at changing the world, but no less effective in modifying their "essence" from the healthy to the moribund range.

There is an interesting implication of these observations for the training of male psychotherapists. It seems true that an effective psychotherapist of whatever theoretical school is adept at establishing a warm, bilaterally communicative relationship with their patients,[25] one characterized by a refraining from manipulation on the part of the therapist. Effective therapists do not "take over" the patient's problems or "solve" them for the patient. Rather, they seem to "be and to let be." This mode of being is quite alien to the average male. Indeed, it can be discerned among beginning therapists that there is often considerable dread of such passivity because it constitutes a threat to masculine identity. Beginning therapists seem to be most fascinated by "manly," active techniques such as hypnosis, reflection, interpretation, etc. —the kinds which will be difficult for them to master, but which will make them feel they are *doing something* to the patient which will get him well. These techniques, however, leave the self of the therapist hidden behind the mask of his professional role, and have limited effectiveness.

MANLINESS AND INCOMPETENCE AT LOVING

Loving, including self-love, entails knowledge of the unique needs and characteristics of the loved person.[32] To know another person calls for empathy *in situ*, the capacity to "imagine the real," and the ability to "let be," that is, to permit and promote the disclosure of being. The receipt of disclosure from another person obviously must enhance one's factual knowledge about him, and also it must improve one's degree of empathy into him. But data obtained in the systematic study of self-disclosure has shown not only that men disclose less to others than women, but also that, of all the diclosure that does go on among people, *women are the recipients of more disclosure than men.*[64] This fact helps one better to understand why men's concepts of the subjective side of other people—of other men as well as of women and children —are often naïve, crude, or downright inaccurate. In fiction men are often alleged to be mystified by the motives for the behavior of others, motives which a woman observer can understand instantly and apparently intuitively. If this conjecture is true, it should follow that men, in spite of good intentions to promote the happiness and growth of others by loving actions, will often "miss the target." That is, they will want to make the other person happy, but their guesses about the actions requisite to the promotion of this goal will be inappropriate, and their actions will appear awkward or crude.

The obverse of this situation is likewise true. If a man is reluctant to make himself known to another person, even to his spouse—because it is not manly thus to be psychologically naked then it follows that *men will be difficult to love.* That is, it will be difficult for a woman or another man to know the immediate present state of the man's self, and his needs will thereby go unmet. Some men are so skilled at dissembling, at "seeming," that even their wives will not know when they are lonely, anxious, or hungering for affection. And the men, blocked by pride, dare not disclose their despair or need.

The situation extends to the realm of self-love. If true love of self implies behavior which will truly meet one's own needs and promote one's own growth, then men who lack profound insight or clear contact with their real selves will be failures at self-loving. Since they do not know what they feel, want, and need (through long practice at repression), men's "essences" will show the results of self-neglect, or harsh treatment of the self by the self.

It is a fact that suicide,[22] mental illness, and death occur sooner and more often among "men whom nobody knows" (that is, among unmarried men, among "lone wolves") than among men who are loved as individual known persons by other individual known persons. Perhaps loving and being loved enables a man to take his life seriously; it makes his life take on value not only to himself but also to his loved ones, thereby adding to its value for him. Moreover, if a man is open to his loved one, it permits two people—he and his loved one—to examine, react to, diagnose, evaluate, and do something constructive about *his* inner experience and his present condition when these fall into the undesirable range. When a man's self is hidden from everybody else, even from a physician, it seems also to become much hidden even from himself, and it permits disease and death to gnaw into his substance without his clear knowledge. Men who are unknown and/or inadequately loved often fall ill, or even die, as if suddenly and without warning, and it is a shock and a surprise to everyone who hears about it. One wonders why people express surprise when they themselves fall ill, or when someone else falls ill or dies, apparently suddenly. If one had direct access to the person's real self, one would have had many earlier signals that the present way of life was generating illness. Perhaps, then, the "inaccessibility" of man, in addition to hampering his insight and empathy, also handicaps him at self-loving, at loving others, and at being loved. If love is a factor that promotes life, then handicap at love, a male characteristic, seems to be another lethal aspect of the male role.

THE MALE ROLE AND DISPIRITATION

Frankl[29, 30] argued that unless a man can see meaning and value in his continuing existence, his morale will deteriorate, his immunity will decrease, and he will sicken more readily, or even commit suicide. Schmale[110] noted that the majority of a sample of patients admitted to a general hospital had suffered some depressing disruption in personal relationships prior to the onset of their symptoms. Extrapolating from many observations and opinions of this sort, I have proposed a theory of inspiritation-dispiritation (see Chapter 10). Broadly paraphrased, this theory holds that, when a man finds hope, meaning, purpose, and value in his existence, he may be said to be "inspirited," and isomorphic brain events weld the organism into its optimal, anti-entropic mode of organization. "Dispiriting" events, perceptions, beliefs, or modes of life tend to weaken this optimum mode of organization (which at once sustains wellness and mediates the fullest, most effective functioning and behavior), and illness is most likely to flourish then. It is as if the body, when a man is dispirited, suddenly becomes an immensely fertile "garden" in which viruses and germs proliferate like jungle vegetation. In inspirited states, viruses and germs find a man's body a very uncongenial milieu for unbridled growth and multiplication.

The male role provides many opportunities for dispiritation to arise. The best example is provided by the data on aging. It is a well-documented observation that men in our society, following retirement, will frequently disintegrate and die not long after they assume their new life of leisure. It would appear that masculine identity and self-esteem—factors in inspiritation for men—are predicated on a narrow base. If men can see themselves as manly, and life as worthwhile, only so long as they are engaged in gainful employment, or are sexually potent or have enviable social status, then clearly these are tenuous bases upon which to ground their existence. It would seem that women can continue to find meaning and raisons d'etre long after men feel useless and unneeded.

5

Sex and Self-Disclosure
In Marriage

Let us talk first about something altogether rare—a married couple
who love one another, not only in the sober sense of loving as
Erich Fromm[32] portrays it, but also in the sense of enjoying each
other, delighting in one another's company. Each knows and cares
for the other, responds to the other's needs, and respects the other's
idiosyncrasies. Neither lover seeks to sculpt the other to conform
to some idealized image. This is love according to Fromm, and,
for that matter, it is love even according to my own unromantic
treatment of the theme.[55] In an earlier book I defined love not so
much as emotion as action undertaken with the aim of fostering
happiness and growth in the person loved. But there is something

grim, even a sense of hard work, implicit in that conception of love. I would like to spice this conception with laughter and whole-some, lusty, mischievous, lecherous, saucy sex. Not sex as mere coupling, but sex as an expression of *joie-de-vivre*, of a sharing of the good things in life. Sex that is deeply enjoyed, freely given and taken, with deep, soul-shaking climaxes, the kind that make a well-married couple look at each other from time to time and wink or grin or become humble at the remembrance of joys past and expectant of those yet to be enjoyed.

Marriage counselors and psychotherapists seldom hear about this kind of sex. While I cannot agree that sex solves anything, it surely is a sensitive gauge of a person or of a relationship. Sex deteriorates with deterioration of the capacity of a person to estab-lish a close, mutually disclosing, nonsexual relationship with another person.

People marry for many reasons, and few people marry for love, because few people are able to love the persons they marry at the time they marry them. In our society, people commonly marry in a romantic haze. They marry an image, not a person. The image is partly a construction of their own needs and fantasies—much like the interpretations people make of a psychologist's ink blots—and partly a result of deliberate contrivance on the part of the other. The other person presents himself as the kind of person he thinks will be loved and accepted, but it is seldom really him. Following the ceremony, reality often sets in with an unpleasant shock. Cer-tainly one of the reasons people marry—and there's really nothing wrong with this reason as such—is for sex. Our morality ensures that many young people will be sexually thwarted at the time they are supposed to marry. This is probably a good thing because it provides a strong motive to bring people together.

Shortly after people are married, trouble begins, and it should if the couple are growing people. Trouble is normal, even desir-able. It begins in bed or is reflected in bed. There are two classes of sexual difficulty, one growing out of prudery and the other stemming from impasses in the overall relationship of a couple.

SEXUAL DIFFICULTIES ARISING FROM PRUDERY

Dread or disgust are readily linked to sexuality in our culture. Young people may be kept in ignorance about the facts of life, or the facts may have been misrepresented to them. They may have heard noisy, fully enjoyed sex play on the part of their parents as part of what Freud called the "primal scene," and misinterpreted the mother's ecstatic groans during climax as evidence of the father's brutality and the mother's agony. Or, the mother may have silently, with martyred air, implied to her daughter what pigs men are and what a cross women have to carry. The father may have warned his son about venereal disease and the horrible ease of making girls pregnant. The daughter may have been shielded from the baser facts of life—though how this is possible today is hard to fathom. Let it suffice to say there is more opportunity for a youngster to grow up associating sexual love with guilt, sin, pain, danger, filth, or disgust than to view it as fun. Let such a person marry. Though prudish, misinformed, or neurotically conditioned, such a person will have sex urges. But a person who is unable gladly to acknowledge his own sexuality will find it difficult to establish the open relationship in which love and sex flourish. Accordingly, the relationship will reach an impasse of sexual frustration for both parties. Since neither one nor the other can get or give full satisfaction in or out of bed, the relationship may be dissolved or freeze into an impasse of impersonal politeness or outright hostility.

To be sexually thwarted is hellish. One cannot work, play, enjoy oneself or another person when frustrated in this basic way. Moreover, sexual frustration in marriage leads to anger and hostility, then to guilt for being angry—a vicious circle difficult to break. Many a marriage that might have had some chance to grow into a loving relationship has foundered on prudery arising from neurosis or ignorance in one spouse or the other. Some wives—latent prudes—close the door on their husbands as soon as the doctor confirms their pregnancy. They justify their action on the seemingly righteous grounds that intercourse will jeopardize the baby. The fact is that intercourse is usually feasible without harm to the baby almost up into the eighth month, if not into the ninth. But many husbands and wives are needlessly abstinent during the wife's pregnancy out of ignorance or prudery. Healthier couples simply proceed until it gets awkward or medically unsafe.

Another outcome of prudery is stereotypy in lovemaking. Healthy spouses are playful. They explore countless variations when they tire of some one position and do so without guilt or shame. It is not necessary to marital happiness to do so, but if the inclination hits one spouse or the other to try something new, the healthier couple explore. And how a prude can spoil such delightful exploration! I have known couples whose relationship deteriorated because one partner was convinced the other was a pervert. The wife became repelled because her husband wanted to kiss her breasts, or he was shocked to learn she entertained fantasies and longing to be more active in foreplay. Naturally, if forepleasures have become ends in themselves, preferred over intercourse, then the individual is neurotic or worse, but as an aspect of sexual love in a good marriage, diverse foreplay is to be encouraged. People who can acknowledge their sexuality in its breadth and depth can usually accept the sexuality of their spouses in its potential diversity.

Ignorance about contraception can ruin sexual lovemaking, although it takes an especial talent today to be that ignorant. Continuous pregnancy is not too good for anybody concerned, though I acknowledge that there are religious and ethical differences regarding the rightness of contraception. As an individual I have no hesitation in affirming my view that contraception is a good thing, the while respecting contrary views of those who affirm over values. Anxiety about unwanted pregnancy can ruin sexual love. Anxiety and sex are mutually exclusive.

Another aspect of lovemaking is aroma. Sex brings people close to one another, to say the least. People stink! Given reasonable cleanliness, there will still be odors. Prudes who reject their own bodies generally are repelled by body odors, especially those musky smells that accompany sex. Healthier couples become even more excited by the odors of love.

RELATIONSHIP IMPASSES AND SEXUAL DIFFICULTIES

A healthy relationship between two loving people is characterized by mutual respect, and freedom to be and to disclose oneself in the presence of the other without contrivance.[55] When two people are thus open, they will likewise be able to be sexually open one with the other. But let an impasse arise, say, an unexpressed resentment, an unresolved argument, something unsaid, a feeling unexpressed, some departure from spontaneous self-disclosure, and it will make sexual lovemaking less fulfilling. Two newly married people who hardly know one another as persons may spend a lot of enjoyable time in bed, but, inevitably, nonsexual aspects of marriage must be faced. As couples come to know one another as persons rather than roleplayers (if they permit that much honest communication to occur), they may learn that they don't like each other or that they have irreconcilable conflicts in values, goals, or needs. The sexual side of their marriage will reflect this state of affairs. Very often the earliest sign that a relationship outside the bedroom is reaching some unexpressed impasse is a cooling of ardor. The optimum in a marriage relationship, as in any relationship between persons, is a relationship between I and Thou, where each partner discloses himself without reserve. This ideal is rarely achieved. In most relationships, it is experienced as moments of rare meeting, of communion. Certainly such moments, when she becomes truly thou, are experienced with joy. When one becomes Thou, he or she becomes unpredictable, spontaneous, and the other becomes likewise spontaneous. At those times sex will be exquisite, a peak experience.[80]

Given reasonable lack of prudery, a lusty sex life grows best out of a relationship between two persons who can disclose themselves to one another without fear of being hurt when they are so unguarded. The same defenses which protect one from being hurt by one's spouse's remarks, deeds, or omissions are the very defenses which impede spontaneity in sex. Openness before a person renders one open to sights, sounds, smells in the world and also open to the riches of one's own feelings. The person who effectively guards himself against pain from the outside just as effectively ensures virtual sexual anesthesia.

One of the enemies of a healthy relationship between two spouses, and thus of any sexual fulfillment in the relationship, is a felt necessity to play formal roles in that relationship. While a division of labor is necessary to the effective functioning of any social system including a family, it does not imply that husbands and wives must constantly be in a formal relationship with each other. When a person marries, is he marrying *that very person* or a wife? If he is marrying a wife, then almost anybody who passes the test will do, because he is marrying a kit of tools and a counter of wares to be used, enjoyed, and consumed. He will pay for the services and enjoyments with money and with services, but this is impersonal. It is only when two people can play their roles, and yet be open, grow, change, that we can say they have a growing relationship. And it is such growing relationships that are compatible with good sex.

Many couples are terrified by change in themselves or their spouses. This dread of growth manifests itself in many forms. One of the earliest signs that a person has outgrown a role in which he has been living is a sense of boredom with his spouse.[50] He feels he has changed, but fears that if he discloses his difference, he will lose love or hurt his spouse. A wife may have been passive, dependent, helpless early in the marriage, and was easily won by a dominant man whose identity as a man was reinforced by her helplessness. In time, she may discover that she has actually become more self-reliant, less eager to please, more able to assert difference. But if she discloses her growth, she may render her spouse very insecure. If she has not consolidated her growth gains, her husband's reactions may frighten her back into the role in which *he* finds her most comfortable. Many marriages threaten to break up and many a sex life gets ruined because one of the spouses has grown more mature. "You aren't the sweet little thing I married," he may say, or, "When I married you, you seemed so strong and sure of yourself. Now, I find that you have weaknesses."

A person who grows raises hell for the spouse who is not growing. And the hell of course spreads to bed. The husband may remain hidden behind the mask of his manly role. The wife may grow discontented with her role before *he* gets dissatisfied with her role. As a matter of fact, it is my experience that problems brought to me as supposedly purely sex problems turn out inevitably to be problems that arise from incomplete self-disclosure. Growth and change in persons who marry is inevitable and desirable. It never proceeds at the same rate or pace in the two partners. Impasses are inevitable and desirable because it is only in facing the impasses that each party keeps his knowledge of the other current and exposes himself to the opportunity to grow. Politeness and the hiding of discontent with one's role or with the behavior of the other are sure ways to destroy a relationship. As a matter of fact, once again we can look to the bedroom for the gauge of the relationship. A couple who harbor undisclosed resentment will fail in the act.

In this chapter, we explored sexuality. The next chapter is concerned with the *experience* of loving.

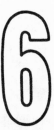

The Experience and
Disclosure of Love

Ol' mas' loves wine, and Miss loves silk, the piggies they love
   buttermilk,
The kiddies love molasses,
   and the ladies love a ladies' man.
   I love to shake a toe with the ladies,
   I love to be a beau to the ladies,
   Long as ever I know sweet sugar from sand,
   I'm bound to be a ladies' man.

Folk song, Southeastern U.S.

Love, O love, O careless love. . . . You see what careless love
   has done.

Folk song, U.S., 19th century

Plaisirs d'amour, ne durent qu'un moment. Chagrins d'amour
durent toute la vie.

Folk song, French, very old

I sowed the seeds of love, and I sowed them in the springtime.
I gathered them up in the morning too soon, while the songbirds
so sweetly sing.

Folk song, British, about 16th century

Amor patriae *Motto*

For the love of God. . . . *Sometimes a prayer, sometimes not*

Eros and *agape. Gemeinschaftsgefühl.* Love as an art. Love as
behavior. The beloved as a "reinforcement magazine."* As sex
object. As an object of worship and reverence. What does it mean
to love? I will discuss love from the perspective of existential
phenomenology.** [70, 71, 77] From this vantage point, love is a state
of being, it is an experience, it is a commitment and it is a
relation.

Who is the lover, and who or what is the beloved? I will focus
on love of persons by persons.

What is a person?

To a biologist, a person is a mammalian organism, a system of
organs. To a general, a person is cannon fodder, a warm body to
carry a rifle, a means to storm a position. To an existential phenomenologist, a person is that which makes a specific view of the
world, time, and space come into being. And a person is an origin
for action which changes the world for himself and for others,
for weal or woe. Further, a person is a situated being who embodies *projects*—plans, inventions, creations—that in time will be

---

*When animals are being trained, the trainer often keeps pellets of food in
a tube, or magazine. The pellets are released to the hungry animal whenever he
behaves as he is supposed to. The food rewards are called "reinforcers."
**Existential phenomenology is the systematic study of a person's way of
experiencing his world. It is concerned with determining how the world which
is common to all is perceived, thought about, remembered, imagined, phan-
tasied, and felt about. I study yours by asking you to disclose yourself to
me. For a more systematic introduction to this discipline, see W. Luijpen's
book, *Existential Phenomenology.*[69]

disclosed for the world to see. Projects are vows, commitments to transform self and world in some way that first exists as imagination, like a work of art.[108] When consummated, they become perceptible to others and to the person who first invented them.

I experience another person in diverse modes. The other person can be likened to a source of disclosure about its being. A tree redundantly discloses its treeness twenty-four hours a day, 365 days a year, to all who would receive these "messages." A person discloses his personality to all who come within his range so long as he lives. To receive these transmissions is another way of saying "perception of the person." I can see, hear, feel, smell, and taste the other, as I can the tree.

But I don't spend all my time perceiving the other. I form a concept of the other, close off my perception, and perceive the disclosures of other beings that exist. Even if I stand before the other, I may not pay attention to his incessant disclosure, because I know enough to contend with him. My questions about him, for the time, are answered.

The other person exists for me perceptually and conceptually. If the other dies, or simply passes from my field of perceptual experience, I can "re-call" him in the recollective mode. And I can imagine him in all possible ways, so that he exists for me in the imaginative mode. I can dream about him. And I can limn him dimly in the phantasy mode, as one who "sucks me dry" or who "fills me."[70, 72] In any or all of these modes for experiencing the other, I can know an affective quality—of joy or sorrow, fear or anger, excitement or depression, erotism or indifference.

The other is my experience of him in diverse modes. But if I touch him, especially if I touch him or if he touches me, he takes on a dimension of reality more real than if I just see or hear him. And he is more real if I smell and taste him. But perhaps he is most real if I touch him. "Touching is believing."

All I experience of the Other is his appearance before my several perceptual systems. But I infer that behind and beyond appearances there is a center, a source that is free. I may try to control and direct his behavior, his appearances, but his center always eludes me. If it does not, he ceases to be a person and becomes a machine or robot.

So to be a person, the other must have a source, a center that he is privy to and I am not.

I can will his freedom, or I can set up the project of trying to destroy this freedom. He will know which of these options is mine by his experience of me. I may be able to conceal or misrepresent my intent for a time, but in more time it will become known to him.

II

I love her. What does this mean? I want her to exist for me and to exist for herself. I want her alive. I want her to be and, moreover, to be in the way that she chooses to be. I want her free. As she discloses her being to me or before my gaze, my existence is enriched. I am more alive. I experience myself in dimensions that she evokes, such that my life is more meaningful and livable.

My beloved is a mystery that I want to make transparent. But the paradox is that I cannot make my beloved do anything. I can only invite and earn the disclosure that makes her transparent. I want to know my beloved. But for me to know, she must show. And for her to show her mysteries to me, she must be assured I will respect them, take delight in them. Whether the mysteries are the feel of her flesh against mine—something I cannot know until it happens—or what she is thinking, imagining, planning or feeling. Why should she disclose herself to me if I am indifferent or if I plan to use her for purposes I conceal from her? She would know me, the one who claims to love her.

If she would know me, then I must wish to be known. I must disclose my being to her, in dialogue, so that we know one another apace.

As soon as she discloses herself to me, I form a concept of her that is instantly out of date, for she has changed. As I reenter dialogue with her, my concept is shattered, and I must form it anew, again and again. If she is free and growing, then she will surprise me, upend my expectancies, "blow" my mind. Hopefully, in ways I like.

If I love her, I love her projects, since she is their source and origin. I may help her if she wants my help; or let her struggle with them unaided if this is meaningful to her. I respect her wishes in the matter.

If I love myself, I love my projects since they are my life. If she loves me, she confirms me in my projects, helps me with them, even if the help consists in leaving me alone. If she tries to control me, she doesn't love me. If I try to control her, I don't love her. I experience her as free and treasure her freedom. I experience myself as free and treasure my freedom.

I am a body. I am embodied. So is she. I like to be embodied, and I like her way of being embodied. If I do not like the way she appears, I tell her, for our love is truth.

I am a sexual being. So is she. Together, we produce an experience that is exquisite for us both. She invites me to know her sexually, and I invite her to know me sexually. We share our erotic possibilities in delight and ecstasy. If she wants me and I don't want her, I cannot lie. My body speaks only truth. And I cannot take her unless she gives herself. Her body cannot lie.

If I see and hear my beloved, I know her more than if I just see her. But if I touch, smell and taste her, I know her still more. But she will not allow me to come that close if she doesn't trust me or want me to know her.

III

I love my friend, and he loves me. He loves a woman, and so do I. He loves his children, I love mine, and I love his. He loves my children, though neither he nor I know the other's so well as we know our own. But I love my friend. I want to know him. We make life richer, more meaningful, more delightful for each other. My life is diminished without my friend being in it. I respect his projects, and he mine. I help him when he wants it, and stand by when he does not. I wish him well in his projects. I know he reciprocates, because he has shown that he does. When he and I talk, there is no semblance between us. He discloses his experience to me in truth—he wants me to know him. And I do likewise. When he wishes to close off conversation, he does so. I respect his privacy. He respects mine. I like the way he "refracts" the world. When he discloses his experience of his world to me, my experience is enriched, because he sees and does things I cannot do directly. Imaginatively, I live more through his experience.

IV

I love my children. They need me. They love in their way, which is not my way. I am essential to their existence, and they know it. I want to help them become less dependent, to be able to cope with problems and challenges without my protection and guidance. And so I watch them and watch over them. I make guesses about how ready they are to be set more free. But I welcome them back when they are hurt or afraid—unless I judge that for them to endure the hurt will help them grow. I want to help, not hinder, the growth of their possibilities. I am often wrong in my judgments, but I mean well. I set them too free too soon sometimes. And I deny them freedom sometimes when they are quite ready to handle it. But I try to get better at my judgments. And they know I intend their freedom and growth.

V

The people I love give meaning to my existence beyond simply filling my gut, feeding my vanity, or giving me pleasure. I treasure them. They help me remain inspirited, turned on to my life. And when they need help, I abandon the projects on which I was then engaged and use my time and resources to help them live more fully, joyously, and meaningfully. They give to me and, just as important, they accept from me. Their acceptance of my giving validates me, enhances my feeling of having worth. I know that I am a worthy being, but I feel more worthy when my existence enhances that of another.

There are billions of people in the world, but I don't love them in the concrete way I love my loved ones. I don't have time. Everybody in the world needs someone to love and to be loved by someone, and I hope it happens. But I am more sensitive to the needs and the disclosures of need uttered by my loved ones. I respond to their cries for help sooner, and in preference to the cries I hear coming from others. This is too bad, but I have to choose. There isn't enough time. I respond to others when I can, with what I can spare from what I have pledged to myself and my more immediate circle of loved ones. If I neglect them in favor of others whom they do not know, I do so because it is meaningful to me. If they love me, and they do—then I expect and receive their patience and confirmation. I have to do what is meaningful to me, and I am entitled to confirmation by my loved ones.

I "tune in" on my loved ones regularly to find out how it is with them. Since last we were in dialogue, a lot has happened to them. My concept of them and their condition is out of date, and I must renew it with fresh disclosures from them, fresh perception. I look, feel and listen.

VI

When I love—myself, family, friends—I see them in a special way. Not as the product of what they have been, of their heredity and schooling, though I notice that. I see them as the embodiment of incredible possibilities. I "see," imaginatively, what they might become if they choose. In fact, in loving them, I may invite them to activate possibilities that they may not have envisioned. I lend them my creative imagination, as it were. If they are weak, I invite them to invent themselves as stronger and to take the steps necessary to actualize their latent strength. If they have been shy or self-concealing, I invite them to try on boldness and self-disclosure for size, to be more creative artists-of-themselves. I too can be the artist-of-myself, if I love myself. And I do. In fact I am the artist of myself to the extent I am aware of my freedom and my responsibility. My situation includes my "facticity" and my freedom.[108] The givens: my past upbringing and present habits, my body, my place, the people I am involved with, the relationships I now have with them and those they want to have with me. All these "givens" can be viewed as exact analogues of paint, canvas and brushes. They are what make me as I now am. As an artist in paint, I can produce pictures that I first imagine, limited only by my skill, imagination, and the plasticity of the medium. As the artist of myself and my world, I can reinvent myself again and again. That is what I usually do, day by day, but my inventions each day are well-nigh a carbon copy of yesterday's. Perhaps this perpetual "rebirth" of myself today in the same way I was yesterday is what the ancient Hindus meant by their concept of *samsara*, the Buddhists with their notion of the "wheel of rebirth," and, more generally, the ages old doctrine of reincarnation.

I can invent a new me in a new world, and strive to bring these into being. If my loved ones love me, they will help me fulfill this new possibility or tell me truly that they don't like it. In fact, they can serve as artistic consultants to help me bring the image into fruition.

I can serve in the same capacities for my loved ones. Inventing and reinventing ourselves, playing with our possibilities, and picking those that please.

VII

My relationship with those whom I love becomes stale and predictable. When it comes to pass that I have no more pleasant surprises and the predictability begins to bore and strangle me, I begin to reflect. What is happening? If the other is my peer, I let him or her know. She reveals that I am neglecting her, spending too much time at work or at play with others. I reveal that our ways of sharing time, satisfying up to last year or last week, are now boring. But she still likes these games. And I like my new ways of spending time, apart from her. We are at an impasse. What will we do? If she does not wish to come along with me, or if I do not want her along, one of us is going to be hurt, and the other guilty. If we love, we have to disclose this. We may have to start to reinvent our relationship. We may, for a time, spend less time with each other, more time with others, feeling somewhat sad and nostalgic for former good times that have passed and are no more.

We may have to reexamine our projects, to see which have lost meaning—our joint projects, and our singular projects. It may happen that, if we cannot invent or discover joint projects that infuse our life together with zest and meaning, we have to go separate ways. This becomes poignant if we are married, because we may decide—one, the other, or both—to become divorced. Or we may discover some new way to be married that looks like a "marriage of convenience"—no passion, not much delight, but some affection, trust, and goodwill. She might take a lover; I might take a mistress. That might be hurtful to all concerned, or perhaps not. If we have loved each other, and still do, the most loving thing to do might be to part, to dissolve the legal connection, and live separate lives with the hope of finding someone new to love. It happens.

There is no end to this chapter, or to loving. Unless, afraid of possible hurt, we decide, not to love, but to control and use.

7

Self-Disclosure, The Writer, and His Reader

There is a distinction between an authentic writer and a propagandist. A propagandist seeks to transmit falsified accounts of reality to people, so that they will form beliefs and attitudes that are useful to the propagandist or to the man who pays this craftsman. The propagandist seeks to diminish people. He has a vested interest in their remaining stupid, misinformed, or uncritical. An authentic writer, whether he be poet, reporter, novelist, essayist, playwright, or short story writer, seeks instead to reveal his personal experience of some aspect of the world in ways that will be understood and reacted to by mature, whole people. He discloses his experiencing in effective or artful ways with no aim other than being faithful to this experiencing. Tacitly or openly, he addresses himself to people who can be enlarged; he wants to enrich their experience. If he makes money or achieves fame through writing, it is because of the accident that, at that time and in that place, people treasure truth when it is artfully presented.

Now I would like to distinguish between experience and self-disclosure. Experience refers to a process—to the flow of feelings, perceptions, memories, and fantasies as these occur from moment to moment. The only person who can ever know a man's experience directly is the individual himself. Whether he reveals this to another person depends upon many factors, as we are beginning to discover. For example, the subject matter to be disclosed, the relation of the audience to the discloser, characteristics of the audience, and individual characteristics of the potential discloser are all factors known to influence whether or not an individual will reveal his experiential flow to another.

Everybody has his unique experience of the world, but some experience it with more intensity of feeling, in new dimensions, and with greater grasp of meaning than others. Hopefully, those who write will be intense experiencers. Literature would be in a sorry state if only those wrote who experienced the world in clichés.

But authentic writing is risky. The chief risk lies in letting other people know how one has experienced the events impinging on one's life. All that other people can ever see of an individual is the expurgated version he discloses through his action. A man's public utterances are often radically different from what he authentically feels and believes. Many of us dread to be known by others as intimately as we know ourselves because we would be divorced, fired, imprisoned, or shot.

A writer may behave in public just like a suburban nonentity and yet record his authentic experiencing in print. In so doing, he runs risks from the reactions of his neighbors, his friends, his family, and others. This is so because if he is true to his calling, that of authentic recorder and reporter of his own experience, he will inevitably show aspects of himself and his personal reactions to others and events that are not ordinarily revealed in everyday behavior. I am sure that the people in the little town in North

Carolina with whom Thomas Wolfe grew up were not aware of the intensity and meaning of his experience of them, and the many lawsuits Wolfe was involved in showed some of the risks of disclosure.

A writer, if he is to be effective, should have a large and sensitive soul. Stated another way, he should be capable of "registering" more facets of the effects of existence upon him than the average person. He must also, of course, have the courage to be, that is, to disclose his experience in spite of censure, risk, economic privation, and the like. I do not like much of what Henry Miller says about Jews, for example, but I believe that he is reporting his experience faithfully and is thereby enriching my experience, helping me to sharpen my sense of my own identity—permitting me to agree, disagree, compare, and contrast my experiencing with him.

This is a curious thing about experiencing which we psychologists are just starting to learn. (We are slow in this respect, lagging behind artists, but we are methodical and steady.) We are learning that sharing one's authentic experiencing with another person has important effects upon both the discloser and the listener. Many a patient undergoing psychotherapy comes to understand his existence and to assume responsibility for its future course as a consequence of revealing himself fully to another human being— his therapist. I have little doubt but that we therapists have lost the chance to make some professional fees because a prospective patient achieved catharsis, insight into and compassion for himself, through writing a poem, a novel, or a play. Disclosure of one's being can be therapeutic.

But by the same token, the person who reads or listens to the hitherto concealed authentic experience of another is enriched by it. To learn of another's experiencing is to broaden and deepen the dimensions of one's own experience. Authentic writing is psychedelic for the reader—it "turns him on." In ways that we do not yet fully understand, at least in a scientific sense, the disclosed experience of the other person enables us to see things, feel things, imagine things, hope for things that we could never even have imagined before we were exposed to the revelations of the discloser. Since we are all similar to one another in basic respects, as well as unique in others, we can understand another's offbeat experiencing if it is fully and effectively disclosed; the vicarious experience that reading or listening provides can shape our essence, change us, just as firsthand experience can. Experience seems to be as transfusable as blood, and it can be as invigorating. Hence, the slogan *Humani nihil a me alienum puto*. Politicians know that shared experience can affect people, and so dictators make pains to exterminate or gag sensitive experiencers who are vocal. They may do this literally, or else render them ineffective by giving them a vested interest in the wealth of the state. More than one good poet, playwright, or novelist has had his experiencing edge blunted by wealth or success; or he has sold his soul for a position on the Book-of-the-Month roster.

Man's capacity to experience the world in subtle and fully described ways is probably the fount of new discovery, both of nature and of man. There was a motto written on the paperback books we bought for philosophy courses when I was an undergraduate—cheap copies of Berkeley, Hume, Locke, and others. The motto read, "To be able to say what other men only think and feel is what makes poets and sages." Now Nabokov, with his account of Humbert in pursuit of Lolita, accentuated in me a dim feeling that would always have been latent and unverbalized and unacknowledged. I never really appreciated the beauty of a nymphet before he called it to my attention. Probably somewhere a young man sits enthralled with the erotic potentials of eighty-five-year-old women, looking for the courage and the art to disclose his experience so that his fellow men can be awakened to a hitherto dim feeling.

One of the magnificent things about Pasternak was his ability to maintain a personal experience of life in a political prison; he saw himself as a person, not a tool of the state. He had the courage to disclose this experience in spite of great risks. Frankl, too, clung to human, personal modes of experiencing in a death camp and resisted the dehumanizing forces present. Authentic writers protect something precious in a people, namely, their capacity to continue experiencing life in personal ways, as persons rather than as functionaries of the state, a business, or a corporation. A writer provides his reader with a role model of both the courage to experience without dimming or repressing this or that facet of self and the courage to share this experiencing with others.

The act of writing bears something in common with the act of love. The writer, at his most productive moments, just flows. He gives of that which is uniquely himself. He makes himself naked, recording his nakedness in the written word. Herein lies some of the terror which frequently freezes a writer, preventing him from producing. Herein, too, lies some of the courage that must be entailed in letting others learn how one has experienced or is experiencing the world. Dried-up writers have confessed to me that they are often impotent in bed, and I suspect that both types of impotence stem from similar reasons. In each case, it stems from a dread of revealing some aspect of the self to one other person, or to a whole reading public. There is a lack of courage to acknowledge some flaw or foible to self and others. The consequence seems to be that, in seeking to block off the flaw, a person blocks off, as well, his creative or his loving flow.

The openness or receptivity to experience so essential to the "'material-gathering" stage of any writing assignment is not so different a mode of experiencing from the openness of a lover to his loved one. A loving man (or woman) opens all his senses, drops his defenses, in order to be maximally affected by his loved one. This is why he can also be hurt by her more than by anyone else. But this is only the intake side of the intake-output equation of writing and loving. The lover responds to his loved one with a spontaneous expression of his authentic being. He does not hold back, but is instead transparent during his transactions with his loved one. By the same token, the writer, at the moment of writing, is making his experience available to his potential audience. If he tries to hold back, it seems he plugs up the verbal flow that must get set down on paper. The difference between the dialogue of love and the attenuated dialogue of writing is that the writer has an opportunity to correct and amend his statement before it gets seen by the world. Incidentally, this disciplined correction may be one of the basic differences between art and verbal diarrhea, or irresponsible self-expressiveness.

I have often wondered about a writer's concept of his reader, as he sits at his table writing of his experience. Does he see his reader as a nitwit, or as an enemy? I think Freud saw his readers as somewhat hostile—perhaps rightly so. I think women's magazine fiction writers and television writers have a contemptuous view of their readers' or viewers' capacities to profit from authentic experience. Certainly, the characters are only paper-thin, with conflicts that fall short of true, human tragedy.

If a writer expresses himself in the way that faithfully conveys his unique experience, his audience will stretch or bend to encounter him. Again, this takes courage, because people, in writing or talking, somehow get the idea that only if they carve the unique edges off their experience and fit it into preconceived molds will they be understand. This attitude denies the capacity of the audience to stretch. Creative people grope for the new forms that will carry their experience; witness the literary experiments of Virginia Woolf, James Joyce, or Kenneth Patchen.

A good question I like to ask of any person, whether he is a writer or of some other calling, is this: Am I diminished, unaffected, or enlarged after my encounter with him? Here are some writers who have enhanced my being and increased my sense of myself and my grasp of the world—Faulkner, Pasternak, Frankl, Kazantzakis, Steinbeck, Hemingway, Camus, Freud, Buber, Carl Rogers, Abe Maslow, Sartre, Arthur Miller, Tennessee Williams, Frank Taylor, Hugh McClennan, Dylan Thomas, and T. S. Eliot. All these writers addressed and enlarged me. I think all of them have been unique experiencers of life and honest and artful portrayers of this experience. They are authentic writers.

The Need For Privacy

We have asserted that people need to disclose themselves for their own good, but they likewise need "private places" if they are to maintain psychological, physical and spiritual well-being. This "private place" may be a physical location, such as a cabin or a "pad," or it may be an ambiance peopled by individuals who share the person's values and ideals. There, he can do or be as he likes, and he does not need to fear external sanctions. Nor need he feel guilt for any discrepancy between the way he appears in public and the way he *is* in private. The only limit upon his action and expression is the rights and wishes of others who may be present, and his concern for his own well-being.

As society becomes more fully urbanized and institutionalizeo, there are fewer and fewer such private places where a person can simply be, rather than be respectable. It seems that only drunks or mental patients in locked wards can be themselves without fear of unforgiving criticism. "They act that way because they are drunk, or mad." But as free space shrinks, the frequency of physical breakdown and withdrawal from social roles (mental illness) may be expected to increase. Or, an entire nation may preserve its present mode of social organization by diverting pent-up aggression to an external enemy. More than one society has avoided collapse or revolution by virtue of a well-timed war.

A society which would endure must draw a sharp distinction between public and private, if for no other reason than to make it a fit society for people to live in, not just for material benefits, but for the rich experience of existence that participation in that society affords.

DISCLOSURE AND CONCEALMENT

Research in self-disclosure, and clinical experience as a psychotherapist provide the basis for the preceding remarks. Let us look more directly at self-disclosure to learn its proper relation to privacy.

The most powerful determiners of self-disclosure thus far discovered are the identity of the person to whom one might disclose himself and the nature and purpose of the relationship between the two people. More specifically, it has been found that disclosure of one's experience is most likely when the other person is perceived as a trustworthy person of good will and/or one who is willing to disclose his experience to the same depth and breadth. In the former instance, the unilateral discloser expects he will benefit in some way if he permits the other person to know him as he is. This is the case in the relationship between a patient and his psychotherapist. Typically, the latter discloses himself to his patient little, if at all, whereas the patient makes his being transparent, hoping that in so doing, the therapist will help him to overcome impasses in his existence.

In ordinary social relationships, disclosure is a reciprocal phenomenon. Participants in dialogue disclose their thoughts, feelings, actions, etc., to the other and are disclosed to in return. I called this reciprocity the "dyadic effect": disclosure begets disclosure.[57] In encounter groups and in group therapy, people gather together in order to drop their facades and present themselves to their fellows in the ways they experience themselves (See Chapter 19). Considerable growth in self-understanding and understanding of others occurs through participation in such groups. But the condition for openness is the guarantee that whatever is presented to the others is disclosed in privacy. The participants feel assured their disclosures will not be betrayed to others who are not present, so that their social image—their being-for-others outside the therapy group or the therapist's office—will remain as it was until the person chooses to disclose more of his authentic being in his usual roles.

Privacy is essential for the disclosure that illumines a man's being-for-himself, changes his being-for-others, and potentiates desirable growth of his personality. Since such healing encounters redound to the benefit of a good society, it is obvious the privacy which is their ground should be guaranteed. Hence, personal counselors and psychotherapists should be guaranteed privileged communication, so they may safely be trusted by those who need to disclose themselves for the sake of their health and growth.

THE SOCIAL RISK OF "PRIVATE PLACES"

Those responsible for leading a society have a vested interested in knowing what people are thinking and doing. Only when the people are thus transparent can the rulers note when there is danger to established order. The various agents of socialization function as representatives of the ideology of the rulers, and they may spy upon people, reporting to the authorities what they have seen. The authorities then can take corrective or punitive steps to ensure present order will be maintained. Thus, parents, school-teachers, ministers, public opinion, and law-enforcement officers all invite or force people to behave in ways they "should" (to keep the status quo), and they impose sanctions upon those who deviate from approved conduct. This is obvious. What is less obvious is that the so-called healers in society, the psychiatrists and psychotherapists, often function in the same, "commissar" fashion. When other agents of socialization have not succeeded in shaping persons to the prescribed roles, the psychotherapists bring their influencing efforts and skill to bear upon the recalcitrant ones and train them to "social acceptability," using the promise of relief from suffering and the implied threat of deprivation of liberty as incentives for such training.

But there can also be healers who may be seen as "subversive." Each time one man reveals himself in privacy to another, a secret society springs into being. If the healer sees himself in the role of teacher or guru (see Chapter 18), rather than as a further agent of socialization, he will aim at helping the sufferer gain a per-spective on the social determiners in his existence and the ways he might transcend them. Just as drugs like lysergic acid or marijuana (see Chapter 14) have a releasing effect upon the consciousness of the user, so teachers and gurus have a "psychedelic" effect upon those who consult with them. True consciousness-expansion (edu-cation) yields a transcultural perspective from which to view one's usual roles and the society within which one enacts them. The person liberated by teacher, or drugs, from unquestioned com-pliance with roles and unquestioned pursuit of social values may be seen by others as a rebel or a revolutionary. As he reveals his expanded consciousness to others, he runs the risk of being seen as a threat to the status quo, whether in his family or in society at large. Thus, authoritarian governments cannot permit psychothera-peutic healers and effective teachers to pursue their work apart from the scrutiny of commissars and informers. Yet, it is doubtful if true wholeness and full flowering of individuality in a nation is possible without the opportunity for consciousness-expansion in privacy, or at least in safe company.

"HELL IS OTHER PEOPLE"

Sartre's[109] statement holds psychological as well as artistic truth. One kind of hell is changelessness. The person who cannot grow, who experiences his own being and the being of the world as "frozen" in its present status, is in hell. Other people can chain one to his present identity by their very modes of relating. A parent, spouse, friend, or authority-figure can exert pressure to keep one behaving, and even experiencing, in ritualistic modes. Freedom *from* the experienced impact of others' physical or psychological presence is the first step in the fulfillment of freedom-to-grow. Artists, writers, scientists and performers who aim at endless actualization of their possibilities attest to the need for solitude. They need it for meditation, rehearsal, and undisturbed pursuit of their ideas. One usually needs to *leave* other people in order to *take leave* of the way one has chronically been with them. This being-with embodies both a pledge from the one person to appear before the others as he has in the past (the ways with which they are familiar and with which they can cope without strain to temselves), and pressure from the others to remain as he has been. "Going away" can be, and usually is, the first step in psychological growth. One need not be in solitude to redefine, or to discover a new being-for-oneself. One can go to a new place, where one's roles have not as yet been congealed in the minds of others. Privacy can be found among crowds of strangers. The problem faced by a person who has less mobility is how to change the concept that others have of him into a new one which encompasses his new phases of growth. Other people—close relatives and friends especially—tend to invalidate new ways of being that are disclosed by someone whom they have long known.[73] They invalidate the growing person because they are threatened by his new incarnations. This is one of the reasons why alcoholics, drug-addicts, and schizophrenics who have been cured (in a new place) frequently relapse when they go home. Others' expectations of them prove more powerful than their redefined being-for-themselves.

OPTING OUT: HIPPIES AND THE INSANE

When young people of the middle classes find that their elders embody roles and ways of life that seem meaningless, they may opt out and commence the hippie way of life. This entails abandoning conventional dress and grooming, avoiding upwardly mobile training or work, and seeking the company of kindred souls. Hippies spend their time in one another's company, listening to music, smoking marijuana, ingesting various psychedelic drugs, engaging in casual love affairs—in short, they have parted from their bourgeois pasts, and they envision no future that differs from their sensuous present. They seek a kind of privacy—an apartness from those "squares" and the law-enforcement officers whom they see as defending the "squares"—in order to live their lives in the ways they find meaningful. This kind of opting out neither benefits nor harms society at large, except indirectly.

Some hippies live lives more in keeping with known requisites of physical and mental health than do their more respectable peers. They live away from the disapproving gaze of their parents, the police, those committed to suburban-bourgeois styles of living, and university administrators. They manage, through a highly developed sensitivity, to know when a "square" is within sight or earshot, at which point they "play it cool," and impersonate current models of role conformity. But when they are in private, they behave with each other in spontaneous, joyous, exploratory, and growth-seeking ways. And they are not socially irresponsible, though some who are less educated may be. They take a keen interest in public affairs, domestic and foreign policy, and standards of justice. But they also seek truth, beauty, and happiness in areas where they are most likely to be found, viz, in honest interpersonal relationships, in nature, etc. Official efforts to root out these pockets of experimental living will, if successful, slow down existential exploration, the necessity for which is increasingly apparent.

Though hippies are seen by "squares" as wastrels, inmates of mental hospitals are a more serious waste of human potential. The mental patients illustrate a kind of privacy, too. The conforming public is spared the sight of socialization failures, who are kept in cold storage. The way mental hospital patients live their daily lives, what they do with their time, is largely unknown to the "sane" public. Perhaps if there were less "privacy" associated with these hospitals, if more novels like Ken Kesey's One Flew over the Cuckoo's Nest[67] were published, new ways for society to treat its failures would be invented.

THE LOSS OF PRIVACY: INSTITUTIONAL LIFE

Hospitals, prisons, military barracks, and live-in schools of all kinds deprive their inhabitants of privacy. This is part of the policy of those delegated to run such establishments, because in unprivateness there is maximum opportunity to control behavior, to produce conformity to assigned roles. Where there is no privacy, there is no or little individuality. It is in such "public" places that Sartre's saying ("Hell is other people.") takes on the most meaning. Authoritarian characters who feel lost without external sources of control and guidance seek institutions that deprive them of privacy, because with privacy comes the awakening of freedom and its attendant responsibilities to direct one's own life. But for sentient, growing persons, institutional life is hellish.

The whole process of becoming a unit in an institution is one of divesting a person of private existence. He no longer has a being-for-himself that has meaning or value to the institutional leaders. His thoughts, feelings, wishes, beliefs are of interest to no one, unless they depart from the approved ideology. He has a being-for-the-institution, he is a "warm body," a source of behavior that may be of use and that must be no trouble to the institution. Beyond this, his being has no value.

In its extreme case, institutional existence is manifested by the totalitarian state or by life in society as Orwell[88] envisioned it in *1984*, where Big Brother could find out what people were doing anywhere simply by flipping a switch. In totalitarian states people whose time can not be accounted for (who have a life concealed from others) are suspected of treasonable activities and are imprisoned. In present-day America, architecture and living arrangements make it extremely difficult for people to find inviolate privacy either for solitude or for unobserved time spent in the company of another person. Men's toilets in barracks and dorms have no doors. Private homes seldom have soundproof rooms; indeed, they are often built on the open plan so that the inhabitants are seldom out of earshot. Lovers seldom have a place to be by themselves, unless it is off somewhere in an automobile or illicitly checking into a hotel or motel. Not to be observed by others by whom one does not wish to be seen can become a desperate, futile, and costly quest in contemporary society. This state of affairs can make a prison or a dormitory out of one's daily living arrangement, producing the feeling that one has been condemned to his usual roles. This experience is most inimical to personal growth, maintenance of physical and psychological health, and orderly nonviolent changes in social structure.

"CHECK-OUT" PLACES

Without the availability of private places, people suffer individually, and society suffers collectively. As a psychotherapist, I am frequently called upon to help people find more viable ways to live than those that have culminated in breakdown. I have advised some seekers to create or find a private place to meditate, to experiment "offstage" with different ways to be, or simply to live without pressure from previous associates who bind them to pathogenic life styles.

From the standpoint of public mental health, I believe a real contribution could be made if the public health officials created in every town a socially acceptable "check-out" place to which people could go whenever they found their daily existence dispiriting. If existing mental hospitals could be demolished and replaced by simple, attractive, modern equivalents of monasteries or by places for new, liberating experiences—centers for personal growth—then the need for the more violent or debilitating forms of psychiatric treatment would vanish.

PART 3

INSPIRITATION AND
WELLNESS

Sickness As Protest

There is growing reason to suspect that hope, purpose, meaning, and direction in life produce and maintain wellness, even in the face of stress, whereas demoralization by the events and conditions of daily existence helps people become ill. Schmale[110] found that forty-one out of forty-two patients admitted to a general hospital during a twenty-three-day period showed evidence of feelings of helplessness or hopelessness shortly before the onset of their various diseases. This loss of morale was typically associated with a disruption in the patient's relationship with a significant other. Schmale reported that such feelings of helplessness or hopelessness may actually set the stage for illness to occur when it does.

In a different study, Canter[15] was able to discriminate suicidal from nonsuicidal psychiatric patients, and between each of these groups and a group of normals, on the basis of scores derived from a personality test. Scores on the test further differentiated between fast and slow recovery from brucellosis and between subjects with histories of frequent medical illness and those with little illness in their backgrounds.

Both these studies represent attempts scientifically to verify impressions long held by laymen and later by physicians, nurses, and psychologists that one's attitude toward life and self are factors both in the onset of illness and in the recovery therefrom. These two studies can serve nicely therefore as a point of departure for a discussion of a revolution which is going on in current thinking about wellness and disease, a revolution that has profound implications for practitioners in the healing professions. Clearly it must have such implications, since the theory of disease and health that is extant during a given epoch more or less serves as a guide to both prevention and rehabilitation.

Schmale's and Canter's studies suggest that if we want to find psychological factors that predispose toward lowered resistance to illness, that foster reduced effectiveness in living, we should look into transactions and events in everyday life that produce a sense of hopelessness, such as a loss of the sense of identity and self-esteem, loneliness-producing events or ways of life, or, more generally, what I call *dispiriting* events.

Let me propose as a general definition that events, relationships, or transactions which give a person a sense of identity, of worth, of hope and of purpose in existence are "inspiriting," while those that make a person feel unimportant, worthless, hopeless, low in self-esteem, isolated, and frustrated, and those that make him feel that existence is absurd and meaningless are "dispiriting." The hypothesis is that dispiriting events render an organism vulnerable to the always present forces of illness,[15, 21, 41, 42] while inspiriting events mobilize the forces of wellness latent in all organisms.

Sickness, whether mental or physical, seems to be one of several ways in which people express protest against a way of life that will not support wellness.[92] People become ill, not just because of germs, viruses, trauma, or stress, but because these assaults fall upon receptive hosts. People become sick because they live sickening ways of life! Hinkle[42] adduced evidence to show that the so-called "normal" ways of life most of us live are interrupted by sickness about ten times a year, the sickness including headaches, colds, flu, diarrhea or constipation, or more serious ailments. Something about the normal or usual way of life must periodically dispirit average people if they become ill with such regularity.

A pertinent question to ask is, "Why aren't people sick all the time?" I think we would find that those people who seldom become sick are people who, although reasonably respectable in their conduct, have found ways of life that permit them to be and to disclose themselves, ways which yield purpose, meaning, hope, interest, and reasonably rich satisfactions of needs for affection, love, sex, status, and achievement. The healthier people, when they find their present ways of life dull, frustrating, or tedious, pay attention to their "all is not well" signals and change what they are doing, including their ways of behaving with others. But this is the joker. It is difficult and anxiety-provoking to change what one is doing, to change or reinvent one's way of interacting with others; powerful forces from within and without tend to restrain change, and so most of us keep up the way of life that has been slowly "doing us in." Therefore, we become sick, and it is usually with some measure of surprise. It is still an unsolved question why the sickness is "physical" for some and "psychiatric" for others. I am coming to suspect that those who are often physically ill are people who commit "altruistic suicide"[22] by slow degrees (see Chapter 11). They are slowly destroying their bodies, as it were, for the preservation of their roles and the social systems in which they regularly participate. They are victims of their sense of duty. The psychiatrically ill seem to resemble rebels without courage or effectiveness.

Being sick is a temporary respite from the dispiriting conditions of our existence up to the onset of the illness. Incidentally, if it seems to a patient that his usual life, the one that made him sick, cannot be changed, he may never get well. Why should he? Or if he does recover but then resumes his usual life, he'll be sick again before long. As he leaves the hospital, we could safely say, and mean it, "Hurry back." If illness has not proceeded too far, when we get sick we merely get into our own beds. If sickness has proceeded to a point where it seems the body or mind cannot restore itself unaided, we then take to the hospital and let the experts have at us.

Medicine has made much progress in describing and labeling the various syndromes of illness; much progress has even been made in identifying the proximate causes of these syndromes and devising pharmacological or surgical methods for neutralizing them. But, it is estimated that except for perhaps 15 percent of all illnesses, rest or change alone will permit the organism to restore itself to the premorbid level of functioning. Official medicine and the media of mass communication have not sufficiently publicized the healing powers of changed conduct, changed surroundings, and rest, and seem to place more faith in the healing powers of drugs.

I have yet to turn on my television set and hear the announcer say, "What do doctors recommend? In a recent survey, three out of four doctors recommended fishing or golf or love as remedies for nagging backache, headache, etc." Who would sponsor such announcements anyway? People have been so brainwashed that they will hardly feel they have been treated *unless* some medicines have been prescribed and ingested or unless they have been cut open. In spite of efforts to minimize the so-called placebo effect in drugs and other therapeutic measures, it has not been possible to state with scientific confidence that medicines heal people. When the evidence is assessed impartially, it seems likely that the patients' *faith* in the healing powers of the doctor, his rituals, his medicines, and his aseptic temples is one true medicine, the other being respite and rest from sickening ways. How else can we account for the many authentic instances of gravely ill people responding to prayer, to proximity to shrines, to chiropractic, to

Christian Science, to the mumbo jumbo of voodoo witch doctors, and to sweet pink pills, and any other symbols of healing power in which people place their faith?

We need to devote our best scientific talent to intensive investigation of the psychophysiological mechanisms which are brought into play when sick people have their faith and confidence inspired by supposed healing symbols and rituals. Actually, we know that healing is rooted in the biological structure of the organism, not in drugs, surgery, or manipulations. We need to identify what might loosely be called the "healing reflexes," part of which are doubtless psychological, and determine what conditions will bring them under the control of either a therapist or the sick person himself. If we had a program devoted to identification of the factors in the so-called placebo effect, to understanding of the relation of faith to healing, just as we did in the case of the development of polio vaccine, we might learn much that is new about illness and recovery therefrom.

The failure of health-scientists to study how healing is promoted by placebos, Christian Science, chiropractic, and the symbols of medical know-how is a fantastic oversight. Perhaps the oversight stems from the effects of propaganda from drug companies. Physicians since time immemorial have noticed that placebos have healing effects.[113] Rather than investigate them rigorously, they have used them, but shamefacedly, viewing the patients who respond to them as stupid, suggestible, or not really sick. Research indicates that the physiological effect of drugs or surgery accounts only for part of the total variance in healing and that perhaps a greater proportion, maybe all, can be accounted for by the attitude toward, and faith in, treatment manifested by or inspired in the patient.[106]

10

Spirit and Wellness

"Spirit" has been a nagging and persistent problem to psychologists. For centuries, nonscientific man insisted that the spirit is real and that it is the essential part, the truly human part, of man. Hard-headed empiricists banish the spirit to limbo time and again, with good reason, and yet the artist, the minister, the layman, all have hung onto this and cognate concepts. Personally, I think many psychologists read and listen to each other too much and do not pay enough attention to what humanists have noticed about man through the ages. I, for one, have gotten interested in taking a fresh look at the concept of spirit in particular, and, following the procedure which Fritz Heider[39] calls "naive psychology," I have begun to look at what is there that is observable and describable when people say, "He is a spirited lad," "Her spirit is broken," "His spirits fell," and so on. Truly, I have found this new "spiritualism" refreshing and, what is rare in psychology, exciting.

Now, when a person is said to have high spirits or to be enthused or inspirited, he probably might also be described as active, expressive, effective in his behavior and of high morale. Probably, when a person says he is in high spirits or feeling good, there are physical, chemical, and neural concomitants to that state. Doubtless, too, there are external, describable conditions that are necessary and sufficient to produce a "high-spirit" response—for example, being told that some significant other loves you or being engaged in effort toward personally worthwhile goals with high expectation of success.

I propose to recall our attention to this mode of being which might be called "highly inspirited," about which we likely have already learned a good deal in other contexts. I will propose some new terms and use some old ones, such as spirit-titre, hope, the general hope syndrome, spirit-responses, and spirit-center.

SPIRIT-TITRE

Let us visualize spirit-titre as varying from zero to 100. At zero, death and dissolution of the body have 100 percent probability. A level of 100 is likely an heuristic limit that can be approached but not reached or, if reached, cannot be sustained for more than a few moments duration—as in the peak experiences which Maslow[80] describes. Probably, most "normal" people (that is, people who live a life of modal, respectable, socially patterned behavior) could be characterized as possessing a spirit-titre somewhere in the range of 30 to 60, with a mode of 45. Let us assert that at this level, modal behavior is possible, but the body is not overly resistant to the ubiquitous germs, viruses, or effects of stress that are the inexorable consequence of the very way of life that is called respectability. Consequently, it could be said with near certainty that "normal" behavior—behavior conforming with the usual age, sex, and occupational roles—regularly yields: (a) social acceptability, or at least avoidance of moral or legal condemnation; (b) status defense or enhancement; (c) minimal gratification of body-system needs (which results in rudimentary increases in spirit-titre); and (d) recurrent illness as we presently define illness.

When spirit-titre falls below some wellness-sustaining level—say around 20 or 30 units—the person is characterized subjectively by low spirits, depression, boredom, diffuse anxiety, or kindred dysphoric psychological states. Simultaneous with the psychological state of affairs, it might be observed that the elegance, precision, and zeal of the person's behavioral output has diminished. Doubtless, in time, the low spirit-titre permits "illness" to take root; microbes or viruses multiply, stress by-products proliferate, latent illnesses become manifest or "galloping."

When people are sick every transaction which the patient carries on with a person, drug, God, chiropractor, or Christian Science practitioner—indeed, whatever inspires *faith*—has beneficial effects, even under so-called double-blind conditions. The "placebo effect" is inevitable, however troublesome it may be to the pharmacologist interested in controlling it or canceling it so as to specify the pure effect of a drug on a tissue or a system.

I would like to propose again as a new discovery what every physician is taught and comes to know through his studies in physiology: that "healing" is rooted in the body-system and that at best the therapists co-operate·with nature. *They do not cure,* nor do their medicines or surgical procedures. Probably the *confidence* which the patient has in the physician (or in the witch doctor, chiropractor, or Lydia Pinkham) is the signal, trigger, occasion, or psychological manifestation of the self-healing "spirit" which welds the body-system into its optimum illness-combating and illness-resisting organization.[84]

Let us now ask the question, what inspirits a person? What

will function so as to increase a person's spirit-titre from the lower to the higher reaches?

INSPIRITATION—SPIRIT-MOBILIZATION—
AT VARIOUS SPIRIT-TITRE LEVELS

Let us consider the problem of inspiritation at the lower levels when a person is sick, even dying. Such persons are generally to be found under medical care in or out of hospitals. We can ask, of course, what was the modal spirit-level of these people during the time prior to their present low level. But let us take them as we find them and see what the typical course of events might be. First of all, the patient is usually now away from a dispiriting, sickness-yielding milieu, and this change of milieu can have inspiriting consequences by itself. Second, he has placed himself in the hands of specialist whom he has been trained to trust. This is notoriously inspiriting. Third, he is looked at, poked, probed, punctured, diag-nosed, dosed, cut open—all of which have both specific situational consequences and also a general inspiriting effect. Selye[112] showed that any stressor has specific noxious effects and sets in motion a more or less stereotyped "general adaption syndrome." The entire medical armamentorium, by contrast, produces specific, local bene-ficent effects, but possibly, too, it sets in motion a general hope syndrome. This may be characterized as a gradually rising titre of spirit which in turn decreases the entropic level of the body-system; that is, it mediates higher-level wellness. When the spirit-titre rises, entropy decreases, and the person's body again is char-actrized by a spirit-titre that mediates "normal" behavior and that often "throws off" symptoms for a time. When the dispiriting forces recur, however, the spirit-titre drops and symptoms recur, which perhaps explains why new therapies and even placebos have only temporary effectiveness.

Sometimes, a patient has no hope, nothing to live for; he has "given up"; his "spirits fall" to a low ebb. When this is observed to happen, of course, a dismal prognosis is indicated. Yet, the history of medicine is replete with examples of "miraculous" recoveries from fatal illness and tissue destruction, where the miracle consisted in a recovery by the patient of the will to live, the discovery that life was worth living, the discovery that people care, that they were praying for his recovery (Arthur Godfrey acknowledged with thanks the prayers which he knew were being offered in his behalf and in which possibly he had confidence). By the same token, less seriously ill people have had their symptoms remitted by placebos in which they had faith and confidence. It may be suggested, then, that all healing is faith healing, in the sense that the patient has faith in what is being done to heal him. This faith triggers off an increase in spirit-titre; the increasing spirit-titre is the signal that healing is going on.

Oddly enough, the people who respond to drug placebos are often regarded or adjudged to be morally inferior, suggestible people who are not even "really" sick. People who get well in response to powerful drug agents somehow are deemed really sick. I see no reason for us to assume that the person who gets well following a drug placebo is any the less sick than someone who responds only to "true medicine." In a way, the placebo-responder may be a luckier person; no matter why he gets sick, his powers of self-healing can be mobilized by substances that are harmless to his organism, whereas the more medically sophisticated have to be dosed with substances that might have directly injurious effects. Possibly, too, the people who respond to powerful medicines are really only highly suspicious people whose spirit and faith has been conditioned, not to the good will of their fellow man, or to pink sugar pills, but only to dangerous drugs.

CONDITIONING THE SPIRIT

If a man's spirit-titre is conditionable, as there seems reason to suspect, then an entire new field opens for investigation. Psychotherapists, physicians, quacks, and witch-doctors all can attest that confidence of the patient in the "powers" of the healer must be inspired if the healing rituals are to work. They do not hesitate to use all manner of symbols that in many instances serve as conditioned stimuli evoking the faith response, which truly does the healing. A good question for us to ask is, what are the unconditioned stimuli which evoke faith, confidence, or an increase in spirit-titre? The assurance of a mother or a father, mediated by cuddling, hugging, or other symbols of protection, care, or effort on one's own behalf—these may be the cues that inspire faith and surges of spirit. We need to discover some empirical response which would permit us to study a sample of spirit by the techniques of the conditioning laboratory.

SPIRIT AND AGING

Let us next consider the phenomenon of collapse, which commonly follows male retirement from productive work. For many men, their spirit-titre has become (through training) conditioned to a certain delimited mode of life, namely, the pursuit, through work, of money, status, or prestige. Their very sense of identity (Is this a psychological counterpart of spirit?) is rooted in their occupational role. When this has been taken away through forcible retirement, it can produce demoralization—being at a loss as to what, of personal value, the individual can do with himself. Under such conditions, depression—loss of spirit—is common, as is the onset of assorted physical and/or psychiatric conditions. It is interesting that women live longer than men, though this mortality differential has not as yet been fully explained. I wonder whether the woman's *role*, in our society at least, does not permit her to be *herself*, her womanly self, even into her 90s, by the simple expedient of training and permitting her to knit, sew, clean, and look after spouse, children, and grandchildren so long as she has a breath in her body. She maintains a lively and concerned interest in the personal affairs of her loved ones. These things—meaningful work and loving, spirited concern—are doubtless inspiriting, and keep the older woman's body as antientropic as her aging tissues permit.

The modal male, on the other hand, cannot consider himself "manly" by doing things that seem trivial to him, the very things that keep his wife vital. He cannot be so "womanly" as to "snoop into the private affairs of others." Doubtless, then, man's spiritual titre drops lower and lower, until he dies—several years before his female compeer. Yet, many older men prepare for retirement, maintaining lively interests, or they have important work which "gives them something to live for"—it keeps their spirit-titre maximal. One thinks of Freud, who lived the last fifteen years or so of his life with a mouth cancer. One wonders whether it was just a "weak" cancer or whether his spirit-level was sufficiently high to so mobilize his body that it contained the cancerous growth within limits that permitted him to continue productive work. The 100-year-old vegetating Civil War generals doubtless had their spirits kept up to the level which sustained life because they felt *their continued existence was wanted and needed,* if for no other reason than that of satisfying the museum passions of the larger population. I wonder, too, whether men in their seventies or eighties who have been obliged to assume "womanly" work—as in taking care of a bedridden wife of kindred age—whether such men are not inspirited, no matter how much they may resent or loathe the work. At least the needs of the helpless partner give them something useful to which they can devote even feeble powers of locomotion, vision for reading, tremulous manual skills for feeding and cleaning, etc. One wonders too whether women who have abandoned much of the traditional woman's role and have become professionals or business-careerists—whether their illness patterns and mean life expectancy are not more similar to that of the modal male.*

*It will be interesting to study these phenomena among women when the various women's liberation organizations make more progress. I am a firm supporter of women in their efforts to conquer sexual discrimination. I hope, however, that well-merited liberation doesn't result in women dying like men. (1970)

SPIRIT AND NORMAL PERSONALITY

Let us now consider inspiration at levels somewhat above those found in the frankly ill. I should like to propose that the so-called normal, "adjusted" person in our society lives a mode of life or behaves typically in ways that keep his spirit-titre considerably below the upper limit. If the upper limit is 100, and a spirit-titre of 30 permits illness to emerge, then perhaps "normal" people function somewhere between about 35 and 55. What this means subjectively is that they seldom know great joy, great enthusiasm, passionate dedication; they seldom function in ways which unfold their productive potential; in terms of sheer work output, they seldom produce much. An intriguing observation is that noted in the now-classic Hawthorne study in industrial psychology[100] Investigators wanted to study the effect of various environmental manipulations on the work output of female workers in a telephone factory. In the crucial test, one group was subjected to brighter illumination in their workroom, while a control group had dimmer lighting. Work output and morale increased in both groups. It would seem that merely being singled out as important enough to be studied removed the *dispiriting* effect of anonymity and impersonality and resulted in an increase in spirit-titre, which in turn facilitated more output. The many subsequent studies of factors in "morale" in military and work situations can readily be interpreted as studies of factors which increase spirit-titre.

Thus, in the average person, the one who is not sick, higher-level (beyond normality) wellness appears to ensue from such events as having one's individuality respected and acknowledged—hence the often beneficial effects of simple, nondirective counseling, i.e., of being listened to with understanding and of being touched. Being heard and touched by another who "cares" seem to reinforce identity, mobilize spirit, and promote self-healing.

Being the recipient of love from another appears to be a highly inspiriting event. There have been many informal observations of people, previously limp, lackluster, dispirited people, who increased in zeal, muscle tonus, integration of personality, and resistance to illness, once they were told they were loved by some significant other person.

At the higher levels of wellness, inspiritation appears to make it possible for a person to actualize all manner of potentialities for inspired performance. An inspiring teacher isn't necessarily a pedagogue well-schooled in the "latest teaching methods." Rather, he mobilizes higher levels of spirit in the pupil, which in turn mediates more focused and effective utilization of energies and problem-solving abilities. Assuming that rudimentary "health habits" are observed, it is doubtless true that more highly inspirited people become ill less often than less-spirited people. People with much to live for, who love deeply and broadly and draw on their inner resources to solve the mysteries of the universe and to satisfy the needs and wants of mankind, probably live longer than less dedicated people. Sorokin[120] found that "saints" lived longer than the mean life expectancy for their time.

What about *reduction* of spirit in the normal person? It is known that, at least among primitive societies, people die when they have been banished from the tribe or when they have learned that a witch doctor has put a hex on them. This probably diminishes spirit-titre to a very low ebb indeed, permitting entropy to maximize.

There is doubtless, too, a class of dispiriting people who maintain their own spirit-level by functioning among others so as to demoralize them, to undermine their faith and confidence in themselves, who literally produce a pain in the neck of the people with whom they come in contact. The comic character, "Joe Btfisk," in "L'il Abner," with his little black cloud following him everywhere, spreads entropy whereever he goes. Superb pianists cannot play a note when he is near, hens don't lay, sick people get sicker. The Yiddish "yenta" and "qvetch" are doubtless similar spirit-droppers and fomenters of the slow heal and galloping disorganization. So too is Stephen Potter's[90] "one-upman." One wonders if the life principle which Freud called "eros," in contrast to "thanatos," does not refer to spirit, as we have been talking about it.

MENTAL ILLNESS AND SPIRIT-TITRE

A given culture offers its citizens a design for living that includes valued goals and specification of means for reaching them. Many of the mentally ill may be regarded as people who have given up the race for culturally meaningful symbols of success. Their spirit-titre has dropped below the level which mediates healthy behavior. Thus, a given culture may require people to avoid behavior which, if engaged in, might yield rich gratification. Or, a given social milieu may be so devoid of opportunities for inspiriting satisfactions of love needs, security needs, esteem needs, sexual needs, etc., that the person becomes demoralized, or dispirited. It is probably possible to assess the spirit-mobilizing or spirit-level-maintaining qualities of a given social structure or a given cultural pattern for living.

Psychotherapy, the deliberate attempt to modify a person's behavior from the range which produces and perpetuates symptoms to a pattern that is both socially acceptable and inspiriting, has not yet been placed on a scientific basis. By this is meant the fact that no one theory of psychotherapy has been proven right while conflicting theories are proven wrong. Instead, accumulating evidence points to a placebo effect even in psychotherapy:[106] those patients are maximally helped by a given regime of psychotherapy who have faith that this technique or this particular practitioner will be of avail to them in their quest for fuller functioning.

The fact was noted above that a person who responds to placebos, a suggestible person, is regarded tacitly by physicians and psychologists as a kind of second-rate citizen. It is curious because, when we reexamine the placebo effect, it amounts to the mobilization of spirit in a person such that his body and personality come to be more efficiently organized against disintegration. This mobilization is accomplished not through pharmaceutical means, but rather through the impact of man on man, mediated through the patient's perceptual-cognitive structure. In short, the interpretation of events (probably a brain phenomenon) is seen to have killing and healing properties which have been observed, but remain largely unplumbed by scientists,[16, 41, 42] though the power of the subjective interpretation has been exploited by primitive witch doctors, as well as by quacks and charlatans in our society.

PRACTICAL AND THEORETICAL IMPLICATIONS OF SPIRIT AND INSPIRITATION

Obviously, we need to understand more about spirit, its dimensions and conditions. It would be most helpful if we could devise indices that would permit estimation of this hypothetical spirit-titre that we have spoken of so glibly. Possibly, neurophysiologists may, at some time, be able to specify the locus of spirit in the brain—and I do not mean a reactivation of the old quest for the site of the soul, as in Descartes' day and earlier.

Practically, there is much to be said for learning the art of inspiritation not only in everyday interpersonal transactions, but also in such professions as medicine, nursing, teaching, and the psychotherapeutic arts. We have, I think, capitalized informally on the "magic" of faith, confidence, prayer, placebos, and so on, but without taking the phenomenon seriously enough as a natural event that warrants study. If it be true, as some psychoanalysts maintain,[33] that God is a symbol of man's never-reached ultimate powers and that man has denied or become alienated from his powers, then if prayer and worship are effective in helping a man reown these powers, we ought to learn more about prayer. If man's powers of healing are rooted in his body, but man doesn't know this and believes instead that the power of healing is "out there" in the physician's black bag, then displaying the black bag perhaps is not the most effective way of mobilizing man's self-healing power, or spirit. I think that once we begin seriously to study spirit as a natural phenomenon, we will not only increase our grasp of nature's laws, but we will radically alter our personal lives.

When a person dies, he is said to have "given up the ghost"; his spirit has departed. Doubtless there is a connection between dispiritation and death from disease or from suicide. I suspect, of course, that there is a connection between the quality of one's relationships with significant other people and dispiritation. In the next chapter, the phenomenon of suicide is examined from this perspective.

11

The Invitation To Die

Personal life resembles the movement of an amoeba through time. Each plan is a pseudopod thrust into tomorrow—five seconds or five years ahead—and man pulls himself into the imaginary world that he thus "projected."

Human life can also be likened to the work of any artist, who, facing empty canvas or shapeless clay, transmutes it into pleasing forms. At first, the picture or statue exists only as the artist's imaginative experience. When he is done, his private image is transformed into a public perception.

Seen from this point of view, man is not a being pushed by drives, pulled by stimuli, or lived by habit. It is more fitting to depict man and his world with *human*, rather than animal or mechanical, metaphors. Man as man lives in a world he experiences—a human world. And man is a body which he experiences —a human body. Man is embodied experience of a world which has meaning for him, like speech. Man speaks to the world, and the world "speaks" meaningfully to him. The world offers invitations, questions, commands, promises, and threats. This is as true of a man's experience of a landscape, a building or the moon's surface as it is of a man's experience of his fellows. Man lives in a world which invites him to live and be in some ways; it directs questions to him; and his world at times invites him to die. A man may accept or decline these invitations. Each man's experience is a possible way for the world to be—an eruption of the world into the human sphere, the realm of speech. "Speak, that I may see thee."[122] Each life is a possible dialogue with the world, a possible series of responses to the invitations, questions, and commands that the world "utters." Moreover, each life, each way to experience, and each way to reply is everyone's possibility. Parrots have no instinctive song; they mimic the sounds about them. Man has no instinctual way to experience and reply to the world's messages. He can copy examples available to him or invent new ways to be. If I can act and experience in some way, so can you.

If human life is the experience of life, he who experiences more, with greater intensity, lives more. If life occurs in time, then he who has more time has more life. If life is experience, then he who would diminish my awareness* is a murderer. And when I blot out my experience, I commit partial suicide.

A person lives as long as he experiences his life as having meaning and value and as long as he has something to live for—meaningful projects that inspirit him and invite him to move into his future.[29, 30] He will continue to live as long as he has hope of fulfilling meanings and values. As soon as meaning, value and hope vanish from a person's experience, he begins to stop living; he begins to die.

Now, I am going to propose that *people destroy themselves in*

* "Experience," "awareness," and "consciousness" can be regarded as synonyms.

response to an invitation originating from others to stop living. And that people *live* in response to the experience of chronic invitations to continue living in some way, or in any possible way. Dying can be seen fruitfully as responses to an invitation, that is, the experience of an invitation. This invitation is extended by others. It originates in someone's consciousness, sometimes as a conscious wish that the person stop existing in that way or at all, sometimes as an unconscious wish, sometimes not so bluntly, but rather as an indifference to the continued existence of the person in question. In whatever mode the wish for death or the indifference to continued existence exists, it is communicated to the one whom we might call the *suicide.* He experiences himself as being invited to stop living, and he obliges. (Actually, he may only be invited to stop that *way* of living).

He may accept the invitation by shooting himself, taking sleeping pills, jumping off a bridge or into the path of a car. Or he may commit suicide more slowly by stopping his projects, disintegrating himself so that he is ostensibly killed by germs and viruses which have killed him because his immunity mechanisms have been called out of action.* Or he commits suicide by suspending his vigilance toward all the things that are always present to kill a person, but which ordinarily he averts or neutralizes when he experiences his existence as having value, when he has things to do, projects to fulfill.

We have enough lethal microorganisms inside us to kill an army, but they usually are held in abeyance as long as the person experiences his life as meaningful and hopeful and valuable. Anything in the world which diminishes a person's experience of hope, meaning, and value to his continued existence releases the activity of the self-destruct mechanisms, faster than ordinary wear and tear will.

I postulate that official views of life expectancy, to which a person has been trained, provide one source of accelerated self-destruction. Thus, many cultures have no role for more than a

---

*A Nobel prize awaits the scientist who tracks down the means by which dispirited states control immunity mechanisms.

few people past a certain age; nor have they the food or shelter for more than a limited number of members of their tribe and group. And so when a person has reached the age at which he is expected to die, if he has been effectively socialized into the world-view of that culture, he obliges by dying. He is assisted in this project by the expectations of others that he will not be around for long. In fact, he may have a dead being in the consciousness of others before he has died (the parallel with voodoo death is obvious). If there is any empirical validity to this analysis—and mean death ages in various societies lend at least some credence to it—then it becomes meaningful to redefine "natural death, from old age" as at once murder and suicide—an invitation to die, extended by others that has been accepted by the victim.

It occurs to me that one approach to the problem of aging people who do not wish to die of boredom or to add to the problem of overpopulation is to create an agency, like an employment agency with international connections specifically for people in their sixties and older. Men and women who have been obliged to retire and who might then age and die rapidly could be given the opportunity to "export" themselves to other places, other countries even, where their knowledge and competence would be welcomed rather than be assessed as obsolete. We already export obsolete munitions, automobiles, buses, and machinery to developing countries.

People who have not been fully socialized and mystified may escape the death sentence by not taking seriously traditional or authoritative views as to the proper time to die; or they may take them seriously, but defy the invitations that they experience.

Our society trains people to expect to live to riper ages than, say, the same society one hundred years earlier. But we kill our citizens in another way—by encouraging them to believe that there is only one identity, one role, one way for them to be, one value for them to fulfill rather than a host of possible "incarnations" to be lived in a lifetime. When this one ground for his existence is outgrown, or lost, a person may begin to die, or he may kill himself more quickly—rather than reinvent himself anew. I have in mind here those people who kill themselves after the loss of money, work, a limb, their beauty, their sexuality, or a loved one or status. I am thinking also of those who, on reflection, discover they no longer are the persons they believed themselves to be. And so, by killing themselves, they are saying, in effect, that they believe they have only one incarnation that is possible for them, one way to live and be. When the ground or value of their existence is eliminated, so is their existence. I suspect that our socialization practices encourage people to believe that they can only be in one way, so that they cannot imagine or invent new purposes, new identities, new lives, when old ones have run their course.

In fact, I believe that most of what we call mental and physical illness is evidence that the way in which the person had been living up to the point of his collapse has truly been outgrown and that it is time for him to stop that way of life and invent a new way which is more compatible with wellness. But members of our healing and helping professions construe the signals that a way of life has been outlived *as an illness to be cured, rather than a call to stop, reflect and meditate, dream, and invent a new self.*

The helping professions do not so much help a person to live as they help him to perpetuate a way of living that has been outgrown. Our ossified theories of disease and health have the sociological function of perpetuating the social, economic, and political status quo. People stay vital, growing, fit, and zestful as a function of the way they live their lives. They live their lives for meaningful projects. When projects are outworn, it is time to re-project, not anesthetize the experience of despair or disinfect the gut; because if the "sick" person resumes the life that was sickening him, it will soon kill him. Can it be that physicians, psychiatrists, social workers, and clergymen help society retain its stability, its present class structure and distribution of wealth and freedom by encouraging people not to reinvent themselves when it is time to? Is it suicidal for a person to consult an established, overly socialized practitioner?

When a person feels he cannot live any more in the way that he has been, when he feels trapped in frozen interpersonal relationships in a social system that he feels offers him no way out, he may fall physically ill, become schizophrenic[70, 72, 73] or psychotically depressed, or he may commit suicide. But the experience of entrapment is just that—an experience. Human consciousness being what it is, it can be mystified and trained in ways that fixate habits of construing; and it can be liberated so that a person, feeling trapped by one way of construing his situation, can untrap himself by an imaginative and creative reconstruing of the situation.[71]

We can ask, how do we typically train people in the activity of construing and in the activity of imagining? My view is that, typically, we train people to an impoverished imagination, a banal image of their possibilities and the possibilities of the world, and rigid ways to attach meaning. We train people to repress their experience of freedom and to replace it with the conviction that in certain situations they "have no choice." Our way of socializing is effective at producing a social system that has an immense productive output and much material wealth, but at the cost of alienating most of us from the experience of our own possibilities. Including the possibility of reinventing ourselves, and reconstruing our situations of felt entrapment. And social institutions such as stupefying television, public education, the popular press, religion, which gain control over people's consciousness contribute to sickness, madness, and self-destruction just as they contribute to maintenance of the status quo. Any teacher who liberates, expands, activates a person's consciousness creates a condition for richer life of longer duration. (See Chapter 13)

The invitation to die, if given in good faith, openly—"Say, why don't you drop dead!"—can be vigorously declined. An invitation to die given in bad faith, as a fantasy wish that is communicated subvocally or that is conveyed as indifference, is more subtle, more difficult for a person to counter. Laing and Esterson[73] were able to document the way family members of schizophrenic girls communicated their wish that the victims annihilate their own view of self and world and replace it with one that was alien. Then the parents denied the part they played in destroying their daughters' perspectives. I suspect we would find that for people who kill themselves, or who die before they "should," we would find evidence of the wish that they die existing at some level of consciousness in the people around them. Or else we would find that the more speedily dying person experiences himself as not existing for others.

The implications that I see in my analysis are to the effect that it is possible to study a social system, or an interpersonal relationship, to see in what ways the invitations to die are communicated, where they originate, and to explore ways to counter them. And it is possible to study socialization practices, medical and healing ideologies and practices, to ascertain in what way they fail to activate a person's experience of his freedom, his creative imagination, and his freedom to reinvent himself when one way of being has palpably become unlivable any longer. Surely there are other alternatives to entrapment than physical illness, psychosis, or suicide.

I think we need in our society to take the precept, "Ye shall be born again" out of Sunday School and put it into our public schools. I think we need to liberalize and pluralize[78] our social structure, so that people can be taught a theory of personal growth that encourages them to let an incarnation die, without killing their embodied selves, so that they can invent new ones and find places and company to live them until they die of being worn out. Meditation and retreat centers,[50] rather than hospitals, where the invitation to live is seriously extended and where guides are available to help a person *kill off the identity he has outgrown* (not his body) so he can invent a new one—these may be an answer to the problem of self-destruction (See Chapter 8). And if we make our society even more pluralistic, people can take a perspective that is unlivable in one scene to another where it is welcomed; or be encouraged to return to their old scenes, but in a reincarnated way. We need to learn how to invite people to explore and try more of their possibilities than modal upbringing seems to foster, so the invitation to live and grow is as fascinating as is the invitation to die. In fact, we need a new specialist—one who helps people find new projects when their old ones, the ones which made life livable, have lost meaning.

One mark of a good theory, as of an enlightened and growing perspective, is its power to reconcile contradiction.[114] A good theory of suicide should make both living-behavior and dying-behavior intelligible. I think that David Bakan's[6] recent book, *Disease, Pain, and Sacrifice*, contains the ingredients of such a theory, one which students of suicide might well examine carefully.

Bakan proposes the concept "deferential" dying to describe the phenomenon of an organism doing to itself what it anticipates and believes the environment is going to do to it. Another term of his, "telic decentralization," refers to a relinquishment of the purposes (*telos*) that give direction and meaning to a person's life (at the phenomenological level), and, isomorphically, permit the organization and form of subordinate processes to operate unchecked by the higher centers. He sees such "decentralization" as a factor in cancer and other physical diseases. The parallel with my theory of "dispiritation" is obvious. Bakan adduces a great deal of empirical evidence to buttress his thesis, and to me it makes sense. Moreover, both his theory and mine have many practical implications. If a person carries within him the means whereby his body can destroy itself and if the environment carries myriad means for destroying a person, the problem to be explained is not suicide or death, but, rather, *living* in the face of so many physical pathogens and so many experiences of invitation to abandon life.

Now, one person can invite another to change his being in many ways. I can invite you to change the meanings you attach to things and events, to reconstrue your world. I can invite you to change from the inauthentic way to the authentic way. I can invite you to buy or sell, etc. It follows that I can invite you to try living in new ways when you have experienced yourself as invited to die. When your purposes have worn out, when it seems that there is no place for you and your way of being a person in a given time and place, and when you feel you have already been abandoned by others, I can invite you to reinvent yourself and find challenge in new projects. You might then become re-inspirited, and attain renewed telic centralization, and renewed life.

Disintegration, or telic decentralization, is posited by Bakan as the condition of self-destruction and as the condition for growth, for further "differentiation" of an organism or a person. Elsewhere[50] I have written of growth as a kind of dying (the end of the tether, the end of projects, giving up, becoming psychotic to some degree) followed by a rebirth—of new challenges and fascinations and invitations. These formulations adumbrate nicely with Bakan's. The suicide, especially the younger suicide, may be seen as one who has reached the end of his tether, of his projects, and who will, unless effectively invited to live, erroneously believe he cannot live further and kill himself.* Therapists would do well to inquire further into the phenomena of invitation and of self-reinvention, since they are matters of life and death.

---

*None of what I have said should be viewed as a moral stand against suicide. I believe everyone has the right to choose his death. But I oppose suicide which arises from failure of nerve and imagination.

PART 4

TOWARD A SOCIETY
FIT FOR HUMAN BEINGS

12

Reinventing Marriage
And The Family

The family is the civilian equivalent of Marine boot camp. It is supposed to prepare people for the combats and joys of life. Let us look at it, however, in the light of the fact that one out of every three spouses checks out of his first attempt at marriage. And let us view the family in light of the hypothesis that rigid conformity to the middle-class design for marriage and family life is the prime cause of physical and psychological breakdown in our time. Many families simply are not fit for their members to live in. The hypothesis asserts that conformity to familial roles produces dispiriting, stressing untenable situations which culminate in physical illness for some and neurotic or psychotic breakdown in others. The role definitions and modes of relating designated "normal" serve more to produce a cosmetic image of family life and to maintain the status quo than they do to foster personal growth and full functioning. Current professional service to families, whether from physicians, social workers, pastoral counselors, or family therapists serves more the function of perpetuating existing family structures with all their pathogenic power, than that of reinventing family structures that maximize zestful life in the participants.[78]

One man, one woman, and no or some children living together in a household separate from others—this is the pattern, or better, cliché, for family life that characterizes the Western industrialized world.

If this design evolved as the most efficient way for people to live in order to keep the economy going and the social structure with its power elite unchanged, the design has been successful. But people at the top have seldom throughout history lived the same pattern of family life as have the larger working majority. Aristocrats and the rich always invented ways to live that scandalized the majority as much as they evoked envy. The conventional family preserves the status quo, but too commonly fails to serve such important functions as facilitating personal growth and self-actualization in the married couple and their children.

As a psychotherapist, I have often been called upon to do family counseling, and I have been struck by the incredible lack of artistry and creativity in the participants. Any one of them may be imaginative in ways to make money or ways to decorate a household, but when it comes to altering the design for their relationships, it is as if their imagination was burnt out. Day after day for years, family members go to sleep with their family drama patterned in one way, a way that perhaps satisfies none—too close, too distant, boring, suffocating—and on awakening next morning, they reinvent the same roles, the same relationships, the same plot, the same scenery, the same victims. There is nothing sacred to the wife about the last way she decorated her house; as soon as it begins to pall, she shuffles things around, changes colors of walls, until the décor pleases her. But the way she and her husband and children interact, long after it has ceased to engender delight, zest and growth, will persist for years unchallenged and unchanged.

Of course, I have likewise been impressed with the same lack of creativity in inventing and reinventing oneself. When a man sleeps his facial expression changes, and the chronic neuromuscular patterns which define his character all dissolve.[95] When he awakens, his facial musculature reproduces the mask that defines his physignomy, he holds his body as he did yesterday, and he behaves toward everyone he encounters as he did yesterday. It is almost as if he pressed a button to release a reproduction of yesterday's self. In principle, he has the possibility of recreating himself at every moment of his waking life. It is difficult, but possible, to reinvent one's identity. Possible, because man is human, the embodiment of freedom; his body and his situation are raw material out of which a way to *be* can be created, just as a sculptor creates forms from his clay. The medium imposes limitations, but the sculptor has many degrees of freedom to create forms, limited only by the extent of his imagination, his courage, and his mastery of technique. But that same sculptor, confronted by the "clay" of his situation, can neither imagine nor make actual new ways for him, her, and them to interact that please, that fulfill needs and values other than the visible *form* of their relationships.

It is possible and difficult to reinvent a relationship. The difficulty has to do with barriers to change that exist in persons and in the environment. If I begin to change my ways of being myself, I feel strange; I feel I am not myself. The different ways of being may make me anxious or guilty. And so I may revert to the familiar, but stultifying, ways of being myself. If I persist in my efforts to reinvent myself, and begin to behave before others in new ways, they may become angered or affrighted. They don't recognize me. And they may punish me in any ways at their disposal for changing a part of their world—namely myself— without first "clearing it" with them. Much invaluable growth and change in persons has been invalidated and destroyed by the untoward reactions of well-intentioned others. Perhaps it is because, if I change a part of their world, the part that I embody, there is an invitation or demand presented to them to change their ways of being. They may not be ready or willing to change their ways. If I lack "ontological security,"[70] I may withdraw my changed being from their gaze. I may wipe out the new version of myself and reproduce the being I used to be in a moment of cowardice. I become an impersonation of a past identity.

When one is involved in a network of relationships like a family, the difficulty in reinventing the relationship is compounded because there are several imaginations, sets of needs, sets of change-possibilities or -improbabilities that are involved. But it is still possible for people of good will to discuss images of possibility, reconcile differences that arise, and then set about trying to actualize them. It is possible to play games*[6] with relationships, to experiment with new forms, until a viable way is evolved. What seems to thwart this kind of interpersonal creativity are failures in imagination on the part of the players, dread of external criticism and sanctions, and dread of change in oneself.

One barrier to change in any institutional form is economics. People have to make a living, and they must find ways to interact with others which facilitate, or at least do not interfere with the necessities of producing goods and maintaining the social, political, and economic status quo. Societies that are under external threat and societies that have an insecure economic base are "one-dimensional" societies.[78] Their techniques for socializing the young and for social control of adults are powerful and uncontestable. Deviation from norms is severely censured of necessity because the security of the whole society is endangered.

But in America, the most affluent nation that ever existed, objective reasons for enforcing conformity are diminishing. At last, we have the power and the wealth (despite protestations from conservative alarmists to the contrary) to ground a fantastically pluralistic society. Indeed, not to capitalize on our increased release from economic necessity and to "play" creatively with such existential forms as marriage, family life, schooling, leisure pur-

---

*The "games people play" need not be as destructive as those described by Eric Berne. One can invent games that liberate, enlighten, and confirm. Encounter groups, properly led, can be settings for such games.

suits, etc., is a kind of madness, a dread of and escape from freedom because of the terror it engenders. The forms of family life that were relevant in rural frontier days or in earlier urban life, that mediated compulsive productivity and produced a mighty industrial complex and immense wealth, are obsolete today.

I think that our divorce rate, and the refusal of many hippies, artists, and intellectuals to live the middle-class model for marriage and family life attests to the obsolescence. In fact, there exists in this nation a great diversity of man-woman, parent-child relationships, but only the middle-class design is legitimized. The other patterns, such as serial polygamy or communal living where the nuclear family is less strong, are viewed with alarm and scorn by the vast conforming majority. The dissenters exist as a kind of underground. But the myriad ways for living married that are secretly being explored by consenting adults in this society and the designs that have existed since time immemorial in foreign and in primitive societies represent a storehouse of tested possibilities that are available to those who would experiment with marriage in our time. Polygamy, polygyny, homosexual marriages, permanent and temporary associations, anything that has been tried in any time and place represents a possible model for existential exploration on the part of men and women who wish or dare to try some new design when the conventional pattern has died for them. Not to legitimize such experimentation and exploration is to make life in our society unlivable for an increasing proportion of the population.

If it is sane and appropriate for people to explore viable ways for men, women, and children to live together such that life is maximally potentiated, then we must ask why it is not being done with more vigor, more openness, and more public interest. We must wonder why divorce laws are so strict, alimony regulations are so punitive, and why people experience the end of one form of family life so catastrophic that they may commit suicide or murder rather than invent new forms and patterns of life.

I suppose it is the task of sociologists to answer this question. But from a clinical and an existential point of view, something can be done.

I have encouraged spouses who find themselves in a dead marriage, but who still find it meaningful to try to live together, to begin a series of experiments in their ways of relating. The image or metaphor that underlies this experimentation is the view of serial polygyamy to the same person. I present the image of two people who marry when they are young, who live a way of relating that gratifies needs and fulfills meaning up to the point of an impasse. One partner or the other finds continuation in that way intolerable. The marriage in its legal form is usually dissolved at that point. But it is also possible that the couple may struggle with the impasse and *evolve a new marriage with each other, one which preserves some of the old pattern that remains viable and which includes change.* This is their second marriage to each other. The end of the first can be likened to a divorce without benefit of the courts. The new marriage, whatever form it takes, will also reach its end. It may last as a viable form for five days or five years, but if both parties are growing people, it must reach its end. Then, there is a period of estrangement, a period of experimentation, and a remarriage in a new way—and so on for as long as continued association with the same spouse remains meaningful for both partners.

Any one of these marriages may look peculiar to an outsider. For example, one marriage of perhaps seven months may take the form of separate domiciles, or weekend visits, or communication through the mails or by telephone. But the idea is that, for growing people, each marriage is, as it were, to a new partner anyway. So long as both partners are growing, they have had a polygamous relationship. The "new" spouse is simply the old spouse grown in some new dimensions.

This model of serial polygamy with the "same" spouse must be viewed as only one of the myriad possibilities for persons who desire marriage to try. The cultural storehouse can also be drawn upon for other models. We could even envision a new profession, that of "marriage-inventor." His job is to develop and catalogue new ways for men and women to cohabit and raise children, so that no one would be at a loss for new forms to try when the old forms have deadened and become deadly. It is curious to me that college courses and textbooks on marriage all turn out to be propaganda for the prevailing cliché of marriage for the middle class. I could invent a course that might be called "experimental marriage," complete with laboratory. The laboratory would consist in households where every conceivable way for men, women, and children to live together would be studied and tested for its viability, its consequences for physical and mental health of the participants, for the economic system, etc. If the prevailing ways of marriage are outmoded and if men find it necessary to live with women, or with somebody on an intimate basis, and if children need parents, then experimentation is called for to make more forms of cohabitation available on an acceptable basis for everybody. The present design is clearly not for everyone.

The criterion of a successful solution to marital and family relationship problems is not the *appearance* of the relationship, but rather the *experience of freedom, confirmation and growth* on the part of the participants. Thus "seeking" spouses can be encouraged to try such things as: living apart from time to time; lending their children to foster parents for a while; trying to be radically honest with one another; etc. So long as the counselor is not himself existentially or professionally committed to *one* image of family life, he can encourage the spouses to explore any and all possibilities, the criterion of their success being not "saving the family" in its present form, but rather a richer, fuller experience of growing existence and honest relationship.

The group structure most effective for fighting an enemy is an army with its platoons and regiments. The group structure most effective for providing care and training to infants, companionship, love, and sex for the adults, and time to work long and hard for material necessities is *some form* of family structure. The family structure for the emerging age of affluence and leisure cannot be prescribed or described in advance, only invented. It is for each couple to commence the project of reinventing their family with imagination and courage

13

Education For
A New Society

I

America is not what it used to be, if indeed it ever was. Whose
perspective on how America is and how it ought to be is to pre-
vail and be defined as "real"? Each person—man or woman, white
or Negro, under thirty or above, rich or poor, in or out of the
Establishment—is a center through whom being is refracted; a
center of orientation for the entire universe, a point of origin for
action. Yet some persons are treated as if their perspective did not
exist, and their action is seen as originating not in their valid and
free consciousness, but elsewhere—their glands, their past, Madi-
son Avenue, or Moscow. But the official view is being eroded.
Perhaps it is impotent.

Negroes are rioting. Debbie—every middle-class family's up-right daughter with shiny hair, flawless complexion, and gleaming white teeth—Debbie pretends to obey her parents, but responds to her peers, and she is on the pill. Growing numbers of boys named Don, who once believed in Horatio Alger, went to church, to school and then into business, are burning draft cards, mari-juana, and their bridges. Women with children are acknowledging the boredom of bridge, the suburbs, kaffee klatsches, and their husbands' conversation, and are going to school, and joining women's leagues for liberation.

The mentally ill are not sick. Those millions sitting in cold storage in state institutions are coming to be seen as other than vessels harboring a disease process, who must be quarantined lest an epidemic spread throughout the land; some of us are coming to see them as "the invalidated".[71, 125] They are those whose very confusion and suffering attests at once to a socialization failure and/or to the unfitness of the officially designated way of life for them. They are unenlightened protestants against a social struc-ture and system that will not fit them. They could be revolution-aries.

The poor are wondering why. The rich are trying to enrich the poor as little as they can so as to minimize the threat to their own positions of power and privilege.

The physically ill are challenging the doctors, asking why they get sick. Is the purpose of illness the enrichment of the medical profession and those pharmaceutical businesses for whom the doctors are sales representatives? Do we get sick because of germs? Or because we live sickening ways of life, ways we could change if we could find viable alternatives, if someone would help us look? Is sickness the hidden price we pay for our way of life?

College students are challenging college administrations. They want responsible "student power" and enlightenment. They want teachers who teach, not trainers who indoctrinate, and they want administrators who will make this possible.

School teachers are striking. They want decent wages, and they want to be treated as grown men and women by principals, school boards, and PTAs.

Clergymen are leaving the churches, and those who leave are neither unintelligent nor mentally ill.

II

Dialogue between generations has broken down. Men over forty are distrusted by those younger. Us.* We run the country, but we are angry and bewildered because our efforts are neither welcomed nor effective. Yet no society can endure which lacks wise men to guide the young and live in loving, respectful harmony with the women. Our society cannot endure in its present form. The perspectives of everyone whom we have hitherto denigrated as one of Them will have to be heard and respected. Who are We? We offer the official view of what is and what ought to be. Anyone who disagrees is insane, a Negro, a woman, a hippie, a Communist, a subversive, too young to understand, or downright evil. Them. We run the government, the great institutions of business, industry, education, the church, and the army. If we became wise and enlightened and humane, we would govern and decide in ways that represent living interests of Them. But we are unwise. We mystify Them, try to get Them to believe that their interests are being served when, in fact, they are not. We exploit Them in order to entrench our own power. Because we are afraid of Them, we don't trust Them, and we are not in good faith.

III

I am afraid that we are producing a police state in the richest nation that ever lived. In the past when previously unheard voices were raised, the people who raised them were often imprisoned or killed to consolidate the power of the ruling elite. But when a nation is as rich as ours in productive capacity, we can at last afford a truly pluralistic society, where many ways to live, be, believe, act, and pass the time can not only be endured, they can

---

*"Us" does not necessarily refer to any particular group, whether of men or women. "Us" is a phenomenological category, a way of experiencing mankind. "Them" refers to all humans who are not in the category of "us."

be welcomed. It is for the production and continuous development of a pluralistic society that I think education, as opposed to training, must come into being.

IV

We have not had education in this nation. We have had institutions which indoctrinate an ideology, a way to experience and a way to behave. The graduates of elementary, high, undergraduate, and graduate schools are not educated men. They are Americans. There is a difference. The source of the curricula in all these training institutes is not knowledge of what men need in order to become transmuted from provincial people with limited perspectives into grown and still growing men of the world. The curricular source has not been philosophical anthropology[11] and humanistic psychology[50]—those disciplines that concern themselves with the question, "What is man at his best? What conditions foster the growth of men rather than the training of technicians and functionaries, people who serve a system?" The ultimate source of our curricula, in my opinion, has been the demands of the business-military-industrial-complex leaders, who by one means or another (mostly money) ensure that those views are inculcated, those views and people are invalidated, and those skills indoctrinated, which will perpetuate the status quo. And so we get a population which is not educated, but one that is trained to do what it must do to keep the system running. A mystified population which believes that the highest purpose of man is to consume goods. A population that believes that our way of organizing society is the bellwether of all mankind. A population with a banalized imagination of what is possible. A people more effectively brainwashed by advertising campaigns, hidden persuaders, and political twaddle than enlightened by teachers.

V

Education like true love cannot be bought. We pay an immense number of dollars each year for schools, and even if we doubled or quadrupled this support, it still would not yield a harvest of *educated* people, because our training institutions are not places for education. And the graduates of these institutions, the taxpayers, do you want, indeed I think they fear, education. Education is a subversive enterprise. It is a process of enlivening the creative imagination, sharpening critical skills, evoking possibilities of thinking, acting, valuing, that may run counter to prevailing orthodoxies. Teachers who show signs of effectiveness at evoking these possibilities in their pupils are rare. They are consistently fired if they are not cunning and self-protective.

The people we wrongly call teachers are graduates of training institutes called Colleges of Education. In my opinion, education seldom happens in these colleges. The "teachers" are trained in the latest means for implementing the latest curricular goals. They are supervised by commissars called principals, supervisors, and superintendants. How can we expect these teachers to educate the young? Moreover, they are badly paid. But even if better paid, there is no reason to expect they would do any more than indoctrinate the young with more vigor and enthusiasm. And if more money is spent for pedagogical hardware, such as programmed instruction devices, audio-visual aids, etc., that will not educate for a new society either. Education of the young calls for a commitment that is conspicuously lacking in this nation. Educated adults insist on education for their children. Trained taxpayers insist on training for their children. There are more trained than educated taxpayers.

VI

Here and there around the country, experiments in *education* have begun. They are true pioneering places. I refer to experimental free colleges and universities, as in Toronto, San Francisco, and New York. There, the courses being taught and the personnel to teach them are selected by the young, by the students. They are saying, thereby, that they don't trust Us, their official elders, to *educate* them in ways that have meaning to them. But more important, I think, than the free universities, are settings like that provided by Esalen Institute in Big Sur, California. That remarkable place is dedicated to the exploration of human potentialities beyond those evoked by modal upbringing and official, institutional training. It is the nearest thing we have in the West to the monasteries and places for retreat and meditation that Eastern nations have built into their social structures for millenia. Seekers go to Esalen to take part in encounters with one another and with Westernized gurus—guides and exemplars to more fully actualized existence. The focus is not upon cognitive knowledge or the cultivation of technical skill in any realm of life or work. The focus is upon the person, the discovery of one's limits to experiencing, action, and human dialogue, and the discovery of those means by which the limits can be transcended.

Esalen pays for itself. It is not tax supported. Seekers pay the fees for seminars and workshops because they feel they are receiving value for money spent. The value is the experience of growing possibilities, of expanding experience, of bodily enlivenment, of enriched imagination and perception, of increased ability to encounter others and sustain dialogue with them. There is no academic credit granted for taking part in Esalen programs. One does not go there to learn the latest techniques for selling goods, manufacturing products, indoctrinating children, curing patients, or investing money for assured income growth. All those things are learned elsewhere. What is being explored at Esalen is the experience of becoming more fully human, of transcending (not subverting) culture. In short, Esalen is an institution for education, not training.

As fast as places like Esalen spring up, there likewise arises the voice and power of the more frightened and hence morally indignant in the establishment: "Arm the police! Shave the hippies! Fire dissenters! Clean up the mess in Berkeley! Teach more Americanism in the schools and universities! Conscript everyone into the army! etc., etc."

VII

The people who go to Esalen are not dropouts. But they do drop out for awhile. They are seekers like Odysseus, who left Ithaca in the hands of women, old men and children, went to see the world, then returned to establish dominion over his kingdom. The full odyssean cycle is to leave home, to open oneself to experience, then to return home, there to make those transmutations which more fully humanize home, making it a more fit place for people to live and grow in.

Esalen-type settings are springing up around the country, a growing embodiment of criticism of the official places for education, places where education does not typically occur—the universities. Growth centers require a material base to support them. The people who go to them pay a fee, a fee they earn through work for which they have been trained in the schools and universities. The training was relevant to develop a nation with the highest productive capacity of any nation that ever existed. But the training did not produce growing men and women, only Americans.

VIII

The new society will be a fascist state, or it will be pluralistic and humanistic. I would like to see it become the latter. There is a very good chance we can make it so, if we mean business. The disaccredited young, who presently live in hippie communities or who are doing Peace Corps work abroad and Vista work at home, the few educated adults, who are materially secure but restless and seeking—these are the people who may humanize and pluralize our society. What role can universities play in actualizing and strengthening a society which confirms not just Our perspective, but the perspective of Them? I think a basic and important one, but it will call for imagination and courage and leadership.

It used to be that the university served the same function for its time that hippieville, Big Sur, and the retreat center serve in our time. It was a place where the elite were released from practical matters, in a sense from the clutch of their culture on their time, experience and behavior, so that they could encounter the great minds and great people who liberated them from situation-boundedness. In America, however, the university, rather than inventing and embodying the future, became debased into simply another place where the system exacted its demands for conformity. The roles of student and professor became as binding as the occupational roles on the outside. In fact, those existential experiments which liberate a person from the clutch of the past so he can invent the future vanished from the universities, and professor and student alike became members of the vast, upward-mobile middle class. Experimentation was confined to crop rotation, training techniques, weapon and productive machinery production; it did not extend to ways of living life, ways of relating to others, ways to organize society. There is no university that I know of where experiments are being conducted in alternatives to monogamous, suburbs-living family life; where Utopias are subjected to study and testing by people who live in them and people who study them. There is no department of any university that I know of where new ways to be a man and woman, parent and spouse, doctor, lawyer, governor, or even thief are being explored and evaluated. There is no university with a cadre of exemplary, "compleat" men and women who can serve as models for emulation, as pioneers along new dimensions of human existence.

IX

What is called for in the universities is not elimination of the training facilities and proliferation of means whereby man's mastery of nature and scarcity can be promulgated. What is called for is the devotion of equal time and personnel to education for the renewal of self and society. We need to "turn on" teachers and administrators through encounter groups, sabbaticals, and other experiences that foster personal growth.

What is called for is exposure of the student not just to a trainer's revelation of his mastery of some field, say, English grammar, chemistry, psychology etc., but also to what all this means to the trainer in the conduct of his life. I would encourage teachers at all levels to disclose to students, not just the syllabus they were hired to dispense, but also their views on politics, ethics, religion, metaphysics, family life, so that students can encounter pluralism in ways of seeing life and living it. I would insist that, even in present-day training institutes, a step toward education could be taken if the trainers were not penalized for showing students the ways in which they are whole men. A Midwestern or Southeastern student can go from cradle to grave without ever meeting a person whose perspective differs from his own.

The problem as I see it is not proliferation of courses. Rather it is a case of those who teach subject matter disclosing to those who learn it *what manner of men they are*. The educational impact of a teacher on a pupil occurs through dialogue, the confrontation of perspectives on all matters where there is difference.

How elegant it would be if those in the teaching professions continued to grow as entire men and women, rather than solely in mastery of the growing information in their specialities. Then pupils of such teachers, from kindergarten through graduate school, would have opportunity to encounter persons with a growing perspective more "psychedelic" than the perspectives of parents and peers. How splendid if teachers went not to summer school to add yet another graduate credit to their credentials, but to a "growth center" for the awakening of more of their human potentialities.

If "teachers colleges" do not teach, but only train, and if we want and need more teachers than trainers, then it would be appropriate to invite members of the profession to *get on with their growth* so that they can encourage, not block, the growth of the coming generations who will be living in and inventing the new society.

14

Psychedelic Drugs: The Impotent Protest

I

When they smoke marijuana and take LSD, I believe young people are declaring how they find prescribed life in this society, how they view their elders—us—our values, our way of life, the role models we are. They are saying they don't like our way of life. They are saying no one listens to them. People with power do listen, but they react with moral indignation and repressive measures, viewing the nondocile young as evil and sick. Moreover, their hair is too long.

This is a context within which I find it meaningful to examine the question of psychedelic drug use.

II

A pharmacologist might claim, "There is no effect upon human experience and physiology that we cannot duplicate with some drug or other." This is more a reality than a boast. There are drugs to numb experience and drugs to intensify it; drugs to put a person to sleep and drugs to awaken him; drugs to intoxicate and drugs to detoxify; drugs to energize and drugs to tranquilize; drugs to expand experience and drugs to eliminate consciousness. They do it fast, but with side- and aftereffects. Like all media—extensions of man—reliance on them robs man of his powers to produce those effects through his way of living his life.[81]

It is appropriate today to assert there is no effect upon a person's condition produced by a drug that cannot be fostered by the impact of man upon man or by the impact of a man's regimen upon his own condition. In fact, I see sedatives as encapsulated caresses and massage. There is no one around to give a loving caress or massage. It takes time, and we have a taboo on touching anyway. I see energizers as inspiriting and inspiring challenges compressed into a pill. There may be no inspiring leaders or challenging work available. I see at least some antibiotics as condensed resting time and prosthetic antibodies, since it is true that, for all but a few infectious conditions, respite from usual activity empowers natural immunity mechanisms to restore healthy balance. We are trained to find rest boring and a waste of time.

I have come to regard the so-called psychedelic substances—lysergic acid, psylocybin, marijuana, mescaline, morning glory seeds, as instant nonattachment and the semblance of enlightenment without benefit of discipline or a guru. They produce massive, unearned detachment from the projects which provide structure to a person's experience of himself and the world, followed by release of all modes of experience from their usual strictures. Since a person is not going anywhere or doing anything when he is unattached, the world and his body disclose themselves to his consciousness in new ways. He has no reasons *not* to perceive, think, imagine, recall, and feel in any way that occurs. The drugs and herbs produce effects upon a man's awareness in an hour or two that are similar to the results produced by meditation, travel, dialogue with teachers, prayer, or fasting.

I believe it is for the want of meaningful work and challenge and future that young people turn on to psychedelic drugs. Just as the lonely, who lack a lover to caress them to sleep, turn to barbiturates. In the midst of the nation with the most immense capacity for producing wealth, we have emptied ourselves of our powers, centered ourselves in our artifacts, and impoverished our experience. We congeal our beings and resist growth. Young people, white and black, not fully emptied, feeling the suffocating impact of mystifying social control, bursting with energy, not yet stupefied by mass media and the public school system, turn to drugs as they turn to false messiahs—for the want of true messiahs and those encounters which evoke growing possibilities and the possibilities of growth.

III

We live in a utopia-for-somebody. It is not utopia for intelligent young middle-class men and women who drop out and become hippies. They are not in dialogue with their elders, but commune if at all with their peer group. It is not utopia for the blacks. It is not utopia for the poor. It is not utopia for many women. For whom is America a utopia? Perhaps just for that minority of men —the power elite and those who are close to them—who profit from the status quo and resist social and institutional and educational change that might diminish their grip on the levers of power. And they are not in dialogue with the many they control rather than serve.

I believe that the use of psychedelic drugs is a nonpolitical, and hence impotent form of protest against the rigidities of the status quo and the lack of good faith or enlightenment of its leaders. It is a declaration that the patterns of life (as these are defined by laws, mores, and institutional leaders) obstruct growth, stultify experience, and engender boredom, anger, or hopelessness.

IV

Official attitudes toward psychedelic drugs and their users resemble "establishment" attitudes toward revolutionaries, dissenters, artists, writers, effective teachers, and anyone who is known to experience the world in novel ways. Legal sanctions against users of LSD and marijuana are just as violent and repressive as the attitudes of censors for the League of Decency against alleged obscenity and of neurotics against experience which would threaten their image of themselves. This should make us wonder.

I believe it is timely to look at users of psychedelic and other drugs not as psychopathological "cases" to be treated; rather, it is time to investigate the drugs and the structures of experience to learn more about them. And it is time to look at the structure of our society, its techniques for controlling and restricting the capacity to experience in the bulk of the population, its techniques for invalidating and gelding different perspectives, both negative dissent and positive proposals for change.[71, 78] These latter include the mental illness sanction, with threats of hospitalization, and the political and social control of research. A more subtle means of invalidating dissent is through the "helping" efforts of psychologists, psychiatarists, physicians, clergymen and social workers. Many practitioners of these "helping professions" identify themselves with the present organization of society. They "help" people to endure and conform to it, rather than see themselves as applied Utopians, spokesmen for the little man, aiming to enlighten and liberate him, to help him to grow in awareness of the forces that control his life for the good of someone other than himself.

V

I believe that *repeated* use of psychedelic drugs has a deleterious effect upon the experience of the user; I can best describe this effect as impaired ability to commit oneself to projects that require time for their consummation. Marijuana and LSD destructure a person's experience of the world, hurling him into the experience of the now. They restructure the experience of time, prolonging the present and rendering the future meaningless. The heightened experience of bodily sensations, the intensified experience of sounds, sights, smells, tastes, imagination, reliving of the past, all are in vivid contrast with the modal experience of the user. Our usual experience is structured by the projects and values to which we are chronically committed. Projects require a person to repress sensory channels and entire modes of experience. These then become intensely activated under the de-projecting effects of the drugs.

Being—everything which exists—can be likened to a transmission center. Everything under the sun discloses its being continuously in many codes and idioms. To receive the disclosures or transmissions of being is to perceive. Perception is selective. We attend to those disclosures of being that are relevant to our needs and projects and are inattentive to all else. While phenomenologists speak of the primacy of perception, man experiences the world in other modes. I remind you of the recollective, the imaginative, the conceptual, and the phantasy modes of experiencing. By means of the recollective mode, we reexperience our past. The imaginative mode allows us to "turn off" incoming perceptual inputs and play creative games, inventing possible perceptions, possible ways for us to be in the world and the world to be for us. If we engage in creative behavior and seek to transmute an imaginative experience of the world (which no other can perceive) into a perception for the other, we are called artists, or simply effective people. The conceptual mode of experiencing the world refers to a way of not perceiving after enough input has arrived for us to classify the world into categories and concepts. If I form a concept of you or myself, I have, as it were, blinded and deafened myself to all disclosures of your being which would challenge this rubric. The phantasy mode of experiencing, which Laing[72] has described, amplifying Freud's pioneering formulations, refers to a way of experiencing being which is available to reflective consciousness only under special circumstances, usually, when it has drastically altered or when it reveals itself to us in dreams and metaphor. We can learn of these several structures and modes of experience through reflection upon our experience as Husserl describes it.[46]

VI

Now, for man, the most immediate determiner of action is his experience. Experience intervenes between stimulus and response. The most immediate determiner of the structure of experience is *projects*, those free commitments to produce an imagined future that provide direction and meaning to human existence. If I know your projects, I can go a long way toward predicting your behavior. If I can persuade or invite you to commit yourself to some projects and not to others, I can influence your experience and your behavior. Your behavior may then serve my interests more than yours. As soon as you are committed to a project, your perceptual experience of the world is affected, as are the other modes for you to experience being. Enculturation practices and techniques of social control are as much directed toward inculcation of projects and the control of experience as they are toward the regulation of behavior. Another name for enculturation is the annihilation of possibilities, or social violence.*[71] Not to share the projects of one's contemporaries is not to experience the world as they do, to march to a different drumbeat, and neither to be able to make sense out of their action nor to be able to infer the experience of which their visible behavior is a function. Hence the incomprehensibility to an average man of the action of a psychotic, a foreigner, a child, a Negro, a woman—everyone we call "Them."

I am coming to believe that psychedelic drug users are trying to detach themselves from the projects and worldviews of their elders, in whom they have lost faith. In so doing, they find themselves projectless. This poses fascinating therapeutic problems.

VII

The world as it is experienced by a person—Lewin[74] called it the life space and the psychological field; Combs[17] calls it the phe-

---

*To be fair, I must also point out that it is only through socialization, or enculturation, that society and some form of culture are possible! The problem is how to socialize people without destroying their more valuable possibilities of growth and self-actualization.

nomenological field—can be likened to a bag or capsule or envelope. I live in my bag, in my world. It is familiar to me. Hopefully, the size of my bag expands—if I let more world in. It may be expanding or it may be stagnant, suffocating. Once I perceive, that is, receive the disclosure of the world outside my bag, I "fit it" into my bag by conceptualizing it, fitting it into concepts and categories. The walls of my bag recede, my world is bigger, I have more freedom to move in it. I can navigate in the world only after I have conceptualized it. I can predict how the beings in my world will perform and behave. If my concepts and expectations are veridical, perception will repeatedly confirm them. This is called reality testing. Concepts and expectations are the experienced dimension of habits, as these are visible to others. Habits are instruments for the fulfillment of projects. If concepts are not veridical, habits will fail to consummate projects, and the person will experience despair, cognitive dissonance, surprise. He is at a point where his experience of his world can expand or, contrariwise, where he can shut off perception, blind himself to the changed being of the world and reassert his invalid concepts and beliefs. If he doesn't grow, he shrinks—the new possibilities revealed in a changed world yield the frightening experience of freedom, and the escape therefrom.

It is relevant to introduce my view of growing experience and the experience of growing.[50] This entails the admission into one's world, one's bag, of fresh inputs of perception that shatter one's concepts, beliefs, and expectations, Such inputs may be experienced as pleasant, exciting, the fulfillment of a hoping consciousness, as in the case of a scientist or an explorer; or they may be experienced as terrifying, as in culture shock, Sunday neurosis, or a "bad" LSD trip. The inputs may originate from one's body or from the world beyond one's body. In any case, reception of these disclosures from the world will expand one's bag, and require one to revise his concepts. If a person re-forms his concepts of being—his own being, and the being of the world, including the alteration of his projects—he emerges with an expanded, brave new world, with the possibility of new projects. He will have grown.

Growing experience and the experience of growth has another dimension besides increased receptivity to the disclosure of the world. I refer here to the activation of experiential modes and qualities that ordinarily are repressed or limited in the service of one's projects. If one is at work on a job or seeking to convince someone of something, he remembers and represses his recall in those ways that serve the project; he imagines and represses imagination in ways that serve the project; he reasons and conceptualizes in ways that serve the project. He even feels and represses feeling in service of the project. Drop projects, as happens with drug use or with dropping out or on Sunday, and the modes and qualities become activated, incredibly enriching one's experience of being. The Sabbath is a primordial "turn-on" time. If a person's capacities to imagine, think and reason, recall, phantasy, and will are activated more fully, he will have started a growth cycle. But new perceptions, memories, phantasies do not yield growth unless a person incorporates these into expanded concepts. This he will do—he will restabilize his world—*only if he forms new projects for the future as compelling as and "larger" than those he has abandoned.* This is where the human problem lies. The projects that are socially sanctioned often are meaningless to the young. They exclude too much of youth's reality, thus the youth "drop out." It is for the older people to pose projects, meaningful challenges, hope for a better world which will turn on the young, or at least not obstruct their explorations. The older people fail because their commitment to the status quo, with their privileged status in it, cripples their imagination and makes mockery of their goodwill. "We'll help as long as we don't have to give up anything." There is an unexplored research and therapeutic problem here: under what conditions will a person invest a project with value?

VIII

Some whiffs of marijuana or about 50 gamma of LSD will desocialize and destructure a person's experience, detaching him from engagement with his chronic projects, the projects which give structure to his experience and make his behavior predictable and conserving of the social status quo.

"Acidheads" and "potheads" often start to read a book, make something, or even go to a destination, but like the Zen man, they get distracted by colors, memories, and phantasies. They stop evaluating the world in the ways to which they have been socialized. The clutch of the taste- and value- molders weakens. An acidhead cannot be depended upon. Since nothing is more important than anything else, he cannot be pinpointed at some place between the beginning and the end of a project extended into time, the way a nonuser can. The "user" is "nowhere," he is situationless. Listening to an exhorting political speech, he is as likely to notice the spittle issuing from the mouth of the speaker as he is to notice the words; and he will not be moved by the words as the speaker hopes and intends. Since he drops out of upward mobility, his earning and spending habits change. He is an economic threat.

One experience that is common to users of psychedelic drugs is the entry into their world of heightened body experience, a magnification effect. Caresses feel keenly sensuous and pleasurable, as between lovers not on drugs who are truly open with one another. The dependency upon drugs to make sexuality more intense and world-shattering and to enliven one's experience of his body affords another example of the deadening effects of our socialization practices. It is also true that loving massage and yoga practices can serve to heighten a person's awareness of his body and recenter him in it. These, however, are time-consuming. Our usual upbringing makes many people become bored or guilty if they take time away from usual projects for these procedures.

IX

I think I understand something of the phenomenological effects of psychedelic drugs on a person during the time he is under their influence. I think I understand something of the longer-range experiential, behavioral, and social consequences. Now, what is my attitude toward their use as a professional psychotherapist?

First, I see reliance upon them, as I have said, as a disclosure by the user that his projects have worn out. His present is stultifying, his future hopeless. Use of the drugs represents an impotent and despairing criticism of the social system and its teachers and leaders. It also represents a failure of opportunity, imagination, or courage on the part of the user to invent new lives or to change the world within which he finds himself confined. Pot and LSD are the poor entrapped man's travel and way to change the world. They differ from alcohol in that after their use the world is not the same. They are not opiates, though they can make a user passive.

The professional challenge is twofold. The first part is seek to ameliorate society so that more ways to live and be are acceptable, validated, and welcomed—to work for a more pluralistic society, through educational, political, and economic reforms. The second is the problem of earning the trust and respect of a user in order to guide him into nondrug ways to expand his experience of the world and to find viable projects that will inspirit him. The latter calls both for an enlightened perspective on society and its ways of invalidating growth and dissent and a commitment to help persons become enlightened and effective. It calls, somehow, for being an exemplar, a role model of a man growing, not just a finished, technically competent middle-class American. It calls for the therapist to become a teacher, a "psychedelic man" able to turn on those whom he encounters, rather than a defender and justifier of the status quo (See Chapter 18, 19).

Elsewhere I have said that a powerful psychedelic event, which does not have the side-effects of marijuana or LSD, is an encounter with a perspective, a consciousness more evolved than one's own. The experience of a more fully grown person, if effectively disclosed to a receptive person, will enliven and expand the world of the recipient. The question is, what agencies in our society regularly turn out such psychedelic teachers? Teacher's colleges? Medical schools? Graduate schools?

To recapitulate: I feel we can best regard the use of psychedelic drugs, especially by the young, as a form of protest, a plaint

which declares that modal upbringing and rigidly conforming ways
of life are unfair and unlivable to many. We do not have a problem of individual psychotherapy so much as a problem of a social
structure that exploits the many for the benefit of a few, while
these few become increasingly adept at mystification and at
anesthetizing people to the pain of social control.

It has been meaningful for me, as one of those seeking new
directions in psychology, to examine the position of psychological
researchers and psychotherapists vis-à-vis the social structure. I
believe that many of us have, in good faith, sought to study man
to help him, only to discover upon reflection that we have been
studying man to help institutional leaders the better to control
him. It is no accident that research in behavioral control is subsidized, research in meditation is not. In fact, research into LSD
and marijuana has drastically been curtailed. As healers, we have
been serving as further agents of social control by encouraging the
"maladjusted" to regard themselves as sick, in need of a cure.
Some physicians are discovering that by prescribing drugs of all
kinds to those who have sickened, they are maintaining the value
of shares in pharmaceutical companies as much as they are helping their patients. It is no accident that research into placebos,
faith healing, and the healing powers of massage or yoga is not
subsidized as heavily as drug research. Some physicians of my
acquaintance have begun to encourage their patients to meditate
upon their lives when sick to discover how they have sickened
themselves, so that, upon healing, they might change their lives
in salutory (for them) ways.

X

Workers in the psychotherapeutic disciplines are commissioned
to foster mental health in a social system which generates alienation, violence, stupefaction, and the annihilation of all growing
possibilities save those that will perpetuate the status quo. No
matter how many more psychiatrists, clinical psychologists, social
workers, and qualified pastoral counselors are trained, there still
will not be enough to cope with the output of despair, crippling,

rage, entrapment, and suffering which our system generates as surely as it produces more hardware than any nation ever has in the history of the human race*

If we know our society produces the need for psychotherapy as surely as it produces racism, then those who are most intimately acquainted with human cost of our social structure should perhaps speak to the humblest voter and taxpayer, and to the decision-making power elite so they will hear. If words, spoken and in print, do not catch attention, then perhaps political action, lobbying, mass resignation, or other deeds of dissent and proposal might. We have a sick-making society, and it is futile to try to patch up its victims because they are generated more speedily than our repair factories can function. There is a sense in which psychotherapists function as agents of short-sighted Establishment leaders, helping to perpetuate a status quo which serves their interests more than the well-being and growth of clients and patients. Perhaps psychedelic drug users and other ineffective protestants against the status quo would trust psychotherapists if they knew "the shrinks" were working toward a more humanized, pluralistic society.

*Dr. George Albee, of the Department of Psychology, Western Reserve University, has documented this point in his studies of the manpower problem in relation to the mental health needs of our society.

PART 5

THE DISCLOSING
PSYCHOTHERAPIST

15

An Invitation
To Authenticity

This entire book can be regarded as an invitation to "authentic being." Authentic being means being oneself, honestly, in one's relations with his fellows. It means taking the first step at dropping pretense, defenses, and duplicity. It means an end to "playing it cool," an end to using one's behavior as a gambit designed to disarm the other fellow, to get him to reveal himself *before* you disclose yourself to him. This invitation is fraught with risk, indeed, it may inspire terror in some. Yet, the hypothesis of the book is to the effect that, while simple honesty with others (and thus to oneself) may produce scars, it is likely to be an effective preventive of both mental illness and certain kinds of physical sickness. Honesty can literally be a health insurance policy.

The invitation of which I speak is intended for everyone, but, being a psychologist, I extend it particularly to my colleagues, both in psychotherapy and in psychological research. I extend it, as well, to others in the healing and helping professions.

I have begun to think about psychotherapy not as a quasi-medical treatment where interpretations are dispensed instead of pills or injections, but rather as an invitational process—perhaps even a temptation. It fascinates me to think of psychotherapy as a situation where the therapist, a "redeemed" or rehabilitated dissembler, invites his patient to try the manly rigors of the authentic way. The patient is most likely to accept the invitation, it has seemed to me, when the therapist is a role model of uncontrived honesty. And when the therapist is authentically a man of goodwill, he comes to be seen as such, and the need for sneaky projective tests or for decoding hidden messages in utterances vanishes. The patient then wants to make himself known, and proceeds to do so. In this defenseless state, the interpretations, suggestions, and advice of the therapist then have maximum, growth-yielding impact on him.

This view of therapy, incidentally, brings it into an interesting relationship with other helping arts. Probably the most effective minister is one who knows sin, who knows the short-run pleasures and longer-run hell of sneaking and who has learned how to find satisfaction and meaning in a more righteous life. Because he knows sin, he can address the sinner with empathy. But he won't get many to accept his invitation unless his very being as a man is living proof that one can be righteous without being joyless, priggish, or bored.

And let us look at the good teacher. Probably he can be seen, without too much strain, as a rehabilitated ignoramus. He has known the hellish smugness of the cliché, the quick answer, the unchallenged certitude; he has known the awe of mystery, and the dread of the unknown—and the adventure of the life of endless inquiry. Since his pupils are presently unenlightened, he knows how to reach them. But they are not likely to accept the invitation to a life of inquiry unless by his very being as a man, the teacher is revealed as a man who has courage and who finds satisfaction and meaning, and even some money, in his life.

So, the good therapist need not have been psychotic or neurotic. These are, after all, only extreme outcomes of a long career as a phony. He need only have been expert at dissemblance, suffered from it, gone through the pangs of reawakened authenticity, and then add technical know-how to his repertoire of responses.

Now what about my colleagues in research? How curious it has seemed to me that our textbooks in psychology are written about man as an habitual *concealer* of himself. I am beginning to think that we, as researchers, have actually fostered self-concealment and inauthenticity in our human subjects, and then reported that human subjects are notoriously duplicitous. Our psychologies of perception, of learning, of motivation, of interpersonal relations have all grown out of research where the investigator has concealed his purposes from the subject, and the latter has likely been in a defensive, self-conscious mode of functioning. What would happen if we began an all-out program of replication, where we repeated all studies previously undertaken with human subjects, but with this change: we regarded the subject as a *collaborator*, and not as an unfortunate substitute for a pigeon, rat, or analogue computer. What would our findings be if we informed our subjects about ourselves, our purposes, our methods, our arguments with colleagues, etc.* Perhaps the subjects would adopt a less defensive mode of functioning, and we might learn a great deal that is new. This seems to be the implication for psychological research of Buber's (1937) poetic dictum, "The I in the primary word *I-Thou* is a different I from that of the primary word *I-It*."

---

*My students and I have followed up this line of inquiry. See References 51 and 57.

16

Dialogue Versus Manipulation In Counseling And Psychotherapy

There is ample evidence today that man can mold the behavior of his fellowman according to some predetermined scheme. We need only point to such phenomena as "teaching machines," Chinese "thought reform," Dale Carnegie's ways of "winning" friends, "hidden persuaders," political propaganda, "subliminal advertisements" on television, and, of course, the centuries-old techniques employed by women to make men see, feel, believe, and do what they want them to and vice versa. The question I wish to explore here is, "Can techniques for the manipulation of behavior, of demonstrated effectiveness in the laboratory, the marketplace, and the boudoir, be deliberately employed in the arts of counseling and psychotherapy?" I will contend that "behavioristic" approaches to counseling and psychotherapy rightly acknowledge man's susceptibility to manipulation by other men, but they ignore the possibly deleterious impact of such manipulation on the whole man. Moreover, the would-be manipulator of a man, whether counselor, therapist, advertiser, politician, propagandist, or woman, may be doing violence not only to his target, but also to himself.

Today, we are almost at the point of being able to program therapy in the same manner that academic learning can be programmed with so-called teaching machines.[116] We are beginning to get some notions of what healthy personality looks like and what health-yielding behavior might be.[48, 55] It is tempting, therefore, to imagine some situation such as a therapist flashing a light or a smile or a glance at the patient whenever the latter emits behavior thought to be health-promoting. If these stimuli have become reinforcing, he thus will increase the rate of wellness-yielding behavior in his presence and weaken those responses which produced and perpetuated symptoms. In fact, if such a procedure were desirable, one might construct an automatic therapy machine, somewhat as follows: whenever the patient talks about subject matter which leaves him "cold' 'and unemotional, a light remains off. The patient's job is to get the light on and keep it on. As soon as he discusses emotionally meaningful material, his autonomic responses will close switches that turn on the light. Shades of 1984! Then, the therapist can go fishing, and the patient will subsequently display healthy behavior whenever he encounters a machine. Monstrous though these ideas sound to me, yet they are not implausible. Greenspoon[38] and numerous workers following his lead have demonstrated the power of a well-placed verbal reinforcer to increase the rate at which selected "verbal operants" are emitted.[68] What is wrong with aiming toward the eventual control of patients' behavior in situ by means of reinforcements deliberately administered by the therapist?

I am afraid that a program of psychotherapy undertaken with such an aim is a contradiction in terms. It cannot achieve the aim of fostering a patient's growth toward healthier personality, one aspect of which, I believe, is healthy interpersonal behavior. It cannot achieve such therapeutic aims purely *because* it constitutes deliberate manipulation of man by man. I believe, and I am not alone in this belief, that man is sick—not just neurotic and psychotic people, but so-called "normal" man too—because he hides his real self in his transactions with others. He relates impersonally to others and to himself. He equates his roles in the social system with his identity, and tries to deny the existence of all real self which is irrelevant to role or self-concept. In my opinion, the aim of psychotherapy is not so much that of remitting salient symptoms as it is that of altering interpersonal behavior from the range which generates the symptoms (manipulating self and others) to a pattern which generates and maintains healthy personality. A convenient name for such growth-yielding behavior is authentic behavior, and it is contrasted with faking, seeming, playacting, or contrived interpersonal behavior—that is, straining after effect, or manipulating oneself in order to appear to be what one is *not*. Such inauthentic behavior engenders sickness.

If we look naively at the psychotherapeutic situation, we observe a patient talking about himself to his therapist. At first, the patient is trying to manipulate the therapist's perceptions of him. But the latter listens and seems to avoid conventional responses to what is told him, such as scolding, shock, scorn, and moral indignation. Encouraged by the lack of expected censure, the patient may go on spontaneously to reveal all manner of things about himself. One gathers he had never before in his life told these things or expressed these feelings to anyone. In fact, in the therapy situation, the patient remembers things which surprise him; he experiences feelings that never before had he even imagined. As time goes on, he becomes remarkably free in expressing what is passing through his mind, and if late in therapy you asked him to describe himself, he would give a much more comprehensive picture of his wishes, feelings, and motives than he might have earlier in the game. Outside the therapy room, people who have known him notice that he has changed in that he seems less tense, more able to acknowledge a broader range of motives, and often much more spontaneous in his behavior with others. Moreover, he seems to be much more "genuine" in his dealings with others. The absence of his symptoms becomes almost incidental in the face of the more basic changes that seem to have gone on.

What has been responsible for these changes which sometimes take place?

The man has gone through a unique experience which evidently *has* changed his behavior from responses that generated and perpetuated "symptoms" to responses which yield more valued outcomes.

This seems to be the experience of being permitted to *be*—to be himself; the experience of being utterly attended to by a professional man who is of goodwill, who seeks to understand him utterly and to communicate both his goodwill and his understanding *as these grow.* It is the experience of feeling free to be and to disclose himself in the presence of another human person whose goodwill is assured, but whose responses are unpredictable. Recent studies[101] have shown that it is not the technique or the theoretical orientation of the therapist which fosters growth of the sort I have been describing. Rather it is the manner of the therapist's *being* when in the presence of the patient. *Effective* therapists seem to follow this implicit hypothesis: If they *are themselves* in the presence of the patient, if they let their patient and themselves be, avoiding *compulsions* to silence, to reflection, to interpretation, to impersonal technique, and kindred character disorders, but instead striving to know their patient, involving themselves in his situation, and then responding to his utterances with their spontaneous selves, this fosters growth. In short, they love their patients. They employ their powers in the service of their patient's well-being and growth, rather than inflict them on him. Somehow there is a difference.

But this loving relationship is a far cry from the impersonal administration of reflections, interpretations, or the equivalent of pellets. The loving therapist is quite free and spontaneous in his relationship; his responses are bound only by his ethics and his judgment. He may laugh, scold, become angry, give advice—in short, break most of the rules laid down in psychotherapy training manuals. This differs sharply from the deliberate restriction of therapist behavior to some range thought to be health-fostering. Such restriction of behavior by therapists makes them the legitimate butt of jokes and caricatures; they become so *predictable*. Evidently it is only the therapist's good will which needs to be predictable, not his specific responses to a patient's disclosures.

It is my growing opinion, somewhat buttressed by accumulating experience in my own therapeutic work, that valued change—growth—in patients is fostered when the therapist is a rather free individual functioning as a person with all of his feelings and fantasies as well as his wits. I am coming to believe that the therapist who strives to remain a thinking, and *only* thinking, creature in the therapeutic situation is a failure at promoting growth. Incidentally, in our concern with what we do to clients and patients we have never asked what we do to ourselves. What is the impact of therapy on the *therapist?* The "technical" therapist is striving to manipulate himself and his patient rather than *respond* to him. He is thus perpetuating his own detachment from most of his real self. He does this by striving to be a good disciple of his master or practitioner of his technique. My patients have been vociferous in deploring those times when I have experimented with manipulation. I have tried limiting my behavior to the dispensing of reflections of feelings. I did a pretty good job of it, too. I have tried imposing the fundamental rule on patients, remaining silent except for well-timed utterance of ex cathedra interpretations. I have, I confess, even tried deliberately to shape my patient's behavior in the therapy hour with some rather ingeniously discovered reinforcers which varied from patient to patient, e.g., the "head-bob" when the output was "right," looking away from the patient's face whenever he was uttering what I thought would be most helpful, and so on. The only trouble with these gimmicks was that in time the patients would "see through them" and become quite angered at being manipulated in those ways.

Patients resent being manipulated. So do I. I become furious when, for example, a salesman gives me a canned pitch which his supervisor told him "worked" in some percentage of cases. I can't stand a Dale Carnegie smile or any of the other departures from simple, spontaneous honesty and revelation of real self in a relationship between man and man. There is something downright degrading in being treated like a boob or a ninny, like something less than fully human. I have come to recognize, too, that those who habitually withhold their real selves from others and instead strive to manipulate them in one way or another do violence to their own integrity as well as to that of their victim. Surely, behavior that doesn't do a bit of good for the therapist can't do much good for his patient.

Buber[10] has succinctly summed up these observations with his concepts of the *I-Thou* relationship and the *dialogue*. Surely, our patients come to us because they have become so estranged from their real selves that they are incapable of making these known to their associates in life. I don't see how we can reacquaint our patients with their real selves by striving to subject them to subtle manipulations and thus to withhold our real selves from them. It reminds me of the sick leading the sick. In point of fact, if my experience means anything, it has shown me that *I can come closest to eliciting and reinforcing authentic behavior in my patient by manifesting it myself.* This presumes that I am able to do this. Probably, by virtue of my own training, and whatever was real in my own therapy, I am better able to do this than an untrained person.

However, my permitting myself to "be real," to be authentic in response to my patient while I am yet committed to his wellness, is a far cry from deliberately sitting down with myself, or a colleague, to plot my strategy for eliciting behavior from him which might make him well. When a therapist is committed to the task of helping a patient grow, he functions as a whole person and not as a disembodied intellect, computer, or reinforcement programmer. He strives to know his patient by hearing him out. He does not limit his behavior to some range prescribed by theory or cookbook. He does, however, retain his separate identity, and he is thus able to see and understand things which the patient cannot. If he spontaneously and honestly conveys his thoughts and reactions, I believe he is not only communicating his concern, but he is also in effect both inviting and "reinforcing" kindred uncontrived behavior in his patient. To a shocking extent, behavior begets its own kind. Manipulation begets countermanipulation. Self-disclosure begets self-disclosure.[51, 57] A therapist who *is* concerned about his patient's lot eventually will be perceived as a man of good will by his patient.

Any man will hide his real self from those thought to be *not* of goodwill. In the presence of a man who *is* of goodwill, even the most defensive will strip themselves naked, so that the other will know their lot and be able to help them. Few women would submit to a medical examination if they thought the physician had voyeuristic motives rather than a desire to know their condition so as to be able to help them. No patient can be expected to drop all his defenses and reveal himself except in the presence of someone who he believes, is *for him*, and not for a theory, dogma, or technique. I believe that the therapist who abandons all attempts to shape his patient's behavior according to some predetermined scheme and instead strives to know and to respond honestly to what he has learned, the therapist who aims at the establishment of a relationship of I and Thou, is doing his job as well as it can be done. That is, if spontaneous honesty between man and man and between a man and himself are worthwhile therapeutic goals. Somehow, I feel that orthodox therapists (we might call them Rogerian, Freudian, or even Skinnerian technicians) are more concerned to verify their respective dogmas than to know and respond to their patients as individual persons. Techniques treat with categories and fictions. Therapy proceeds through honest responses to this very person *by this very person.*

17

Resistance To Authenticity In The Psychotherapist

One of Freud's monumental contributions to the art and science of psychotherapy was his discovery and elucidation of resistance and transference in the patient. As time went on, therapy came better to be understood as a dyadic transaction rather than as a monologue by the patient, with the person of the therapist hidden behind interpretations and the couch. One outcome of this realization was recognition of the countertransference. Today, most therapists are prepared to examine and reflect upon their own feelings and thoughts as they ebb and flow in the course of therapy.

But there is another phenomenon that arises in the therapist just as surely as it arises in the patient. I am referring now to what may be called *resistance to authentic being* in the therapist. Just as a patient will pick and choose his utterances for their intended effect on the therapist (a violation of Freud's fundamental rule), so will a therapist often pick and choose his behavior for its supposed effect on the patient. This I now see as a violation of what may become a fundamental rule for the therapist: that he should be spontaneously open in response to the patient. Resistance to being, to being oneself with the patient, seems to be quite as characteristic of beginning therapists and of more experienced "technicians" of therapy as it is of patients and often for similar reasons, i.e., latent fear of how one will seem to the other as well as how one will seem to oneself, or dread of what will happen if one "lets go" of one's tight self-control.

In its starkest, most operational meaning, resistance in a patient refers to his reluctance or inability to disclose his thoughts, fantasies, feelings, or memories as these spontaneously arise in the therapeutic session. Rather than make himself known, the patient tries to manipulate his own disclosing behavior so as to shape the therapist's perceptions, feelings, and attitudes.

Just as the patient's ongoing stream of associations may be blocked by anxiety or picked over for some desired impact on the therapist, so may the therapist's utterances. The therapist may practice what Buber[11] calls "semblance," or "seeming," as chronically as does the patient. This I suspect is inimical to growth of self in *both* parties. It has often happened that a patient has asked what I thought about him, or how I felt about him. Earlier, I would automatically reflect or restate his question or try to understand and then expound my opinion of his motives for asking. In technical terms, I was probably correct in responding to him in these ways, but I have now come to suspect that anxiety about disclosing to the patient what one thinks or feels about him may be one of the many forms of resistance to authenticity and resistance to growth in the therapist, just as the patient's dread or inability to reveal his thoughts as they arise is resistance.

Hora,[43] speaking of existential psychotherapy, states,
The existential psychotherapist does not "do" psychotherapy, he

lives it. He meets his patient in the openness of an interhuman existential encounter. He does not seek to make interpretations, he does not evaluate and judge; *he allows what is to be, so that it can reveal itself in the essence of its being, and then proceeds to elucidate what he understands.*

In somewhat similar, but not identical vein, I have come gradually to see therapy not as a setting in which one person, the therapist, *does things to a patient,* manipulating the relationship, the patient's behavior, or his own to make the patient get well or grow, but rather as a relationship that can be described in Buber's terminology—namely, an honest relationship gradually developing into one of I and Thou; a dialogue, in which growth of both parties is an outcome. I now suspect that the enforced discipline of making reflections or interpretations is behavior from the therapist that is not only of limited value to the patient, but is likewise confining for the therapist. An example will show what I mean by this. I have often found that following a number of therapeutic sessions I would be exhausted and sometimes afflicted with a headache—symptoms that are common among people who have been forced to suppress or withhold spontaneous experience from disclosure in a face-to-face situation. Yet, as I reviewed the notes or recording or my memory of the sessions, I would discover that my behavior as a therapist had been technically faultless and had done the patient no harm. But I could also say in all honesty that my behavior had done no perceptible good either, for him or for me. I reasoned, "Surely behavior that does me harm can't be good for the patient." My technically correct behavior was in some sense defensive; and it seemed to impede my own growth as well as the patient's. I then wondered why I was so tense and exhausted. It soon became clear that my exhaustion came from withholding myself from my patient, from my own resistances to authentic being and, I am now inclined to say, to growing.

With this realization, many recollections came rushing to me of patients who had begged me to tell them what I thought, only to be met by my cool, faultless reflection or interpretation of their question or else by a downright lie, e.g., "Yes, I like you," when in fact I found them boring or unlikable. Also, there came to me recollections of instances where I had violated what I thought were technical rules, for example, holding a weeping patient's hand or bursting out laughing at something the patient had said, and of patients later telling me that when I had done things, I somehow became human, a person, and that these were significant moments for the patients in the course of their therapy.[50, 123]

My behavior as a therapist has changed slowly, but radically, over the years. I am as good a listener as I ever was, perhaps better. My capacity for empathy and my overall judgment are greater now than they were earlier. I reflect feelings and content as I always did, but only when I want the patient to know what I heard him say. In fact, I agree with Rogers that there is no better way to tell a patient you heard him, and this acknowledged listening seems to reinforce further disclosing of *his* being by him. But I find myself sometimes giving advice, lecturing, laughing, becoming angry, interpreting, telling my fantasies, asking questions—in short, doing whatever occurs to me *during* the therapeutic session in response to the other person. This change could mean either that I am growing as a person and as a therapist or else that, through lack of close supervision, I am losing in "discipline." Yet, I do discuss my work with colleagues, and I am not isolated.

My actual disclosures to the patient are still checked by common sense or by my judgment (I sometimes suspect that this is automatic and unconscious checking, though I realize this sounds mystical), but increasingly I find myself being more unpremeditated and spontaneous in my responses to the patient. It is as if I am coming more to trust myself, as if I trust that what comes out of me in response to a patient will not harm him or create a situation with which I cannot cope. This does not mean I am anti-intellectual, because I am not. Rather, it seems that, just as I can hear with a "third ear," I can sometimes listen to my "second voice"—the voice of my spontaneous response. Perhaps here we have the active counterpart to Theodore Reik's[96] classic, *Listening* with the Third Ear, namely, "Speaking with the Second Voice."*

When I become strictly technical and hence impersonal with my patients, I have learned it is usually because I have become anxious. When I am lucky enough to recognize my anxiety, I will sometimes say, "You are making me anxious." If I am angry, I let this be known. If I am concerned or worried, I let this be known.

If a patient asks me a question that I genuinely would rather not answer, I tell him, "I'd rather not answer." I give him true reasons, too. The most succinct way I have of describing what I do is that I strive to give the patient an openness of myself in that moment. I believe that he is entitled to an honest expression of myself as a professional man, and this is what I give him. This is the transparency, the "congruence," which Rogers has so lucidly described.[101, 102] He states, for example,

> Congruence is the opposite of presenting a facade, a defensive front, to the patient or client. If the therapist is experiencing one thing in the relationship, but is endeavoring to be something else, then the condition (of congruence) is not met. . . . To be transparent to the client, to have nothing of one's experience in the *relationship* which is hidden . . . this is, I believe, basic to effective psychotherapy. . . . The therapist, by being openly and freely himself, is ready for and is offering the possibility of an existential encounter between two real persons. . . . (It) is these moments, I believe, which are theraputic.

Buber,[11] speaking of genuine dialogue, states that

> If genuine dialogue is to arise, everyone who takes part in it must bring himself into it. . . . He must be willing on each occasion to say what is really in his mind about the subject of the conversation. . . . No one . . . *can know in advance what it is that he has to say.*

*If spontaneous disclosure occurs, developmentally, before contrived disclosure, then it might be more accurate to regard technical responses from a therapist as the "second voice," and spontaneous utterance as the "first."

The question then arises, why not be thus spontaneous and open? There are many objections that come to mind. One grows from what I believe is *the assumption that it is technique as such which promotes growth or wellness in a patient*, and there is really no evidence I know of to support such an assumption, unless it lies in the data which deals with the placebo effect. Doubtless technical behavior impresses patients who are impressible by such "magic"—and we should not lightly dismiss the value of magic. We still do not understand the psychological and neurological mechanisms of faith, hope, and charisma! Fiedler's[25] studies and Eysenck's[24] cast grave doubt on the healing powers of technique per se. Technique, including reflection, silence, interpretation, seems to function as a defense against immature being, and it is doubtless valuable for that reason. Furthermore, it is often a safe or harmless way to interact and hence has value for that purpose. Finally, technique can be taught.

Another objection to openness is that therapists may fear that in being their real selves in the therapeutic session they may harm the patient or "act out" in various ways. Or they may reveal their authentic immaturity or ineptitude. The patient may then go elsewhere for help—not such a bad thing after all, if he is not getting understanding and growth-yielding behavior from the therapist. I don't think expert technique can long hide immaturity, anxiety, hostility, sexuality, if these exist in the therapist. Patients are seldom that insensitive. Moreover, if a therapist thus hides his being, he is engaging in the same inauthentic behavior that generated symptoms in the patient, and supposedly, he is trying to undo this self-alienating process.

The spontaneous dialogue in which a therapist can engage with his patients (if he dares) seems to result in the outcome that the patient will come to know him *as he is during the hours together.* (One need not tell the patient about one's life outside the therapy hour, unless one wishes.) This serves, among other things, gradually to correct the patient's transference misperceptions as they arise. Furthermore, spontaneity makes the therapist's reponses unpredictable and uncontrollable by the patient. This tends to "up-end" many of his expectancies, in Frank Shaw's[114] terms, and also helps extinguish omnipotence fantasies that arise in chronic manipulators.

Another outcome is that the therapist's openness serves gradually to relieve the patient's distrust, something which most patients bring with them into therapy. Still another outcome is that the therapist, by being open, by letting himself be as well as he lets the patient be, provides the patient with a role model of authentic being with which he can identify. Many a patient has ended orthodox psychoanalytic, or client-centered, therapy as a good listener, as a reflector of feelings or a dispenser of theoretically sound interpretations of his own or other's behavior, but such persons seldom make themselves very popular. Not that popularity is a desired outcome to therapy. But they have acquired these traits through mimicry, through identification with the behavior of their therapists. Since identification does occur, we may as well provide a wholesome, authentic model.[130] As Jung[66] says, "Be the man through whom you wish to influence others."

Spontaneous disclosure by the therapist of his authentic experience during a session does not mean that therapists should stop using technique, making diagnoses, or using judgment, but rather that they will frequently think out loud, or else tell the patient frankly that they do not want to express their thinking right now.

Some Signs of Resistance in the Therapist
1. Having fantasies during the session, and not disclosing them.
2. Chronically giving technical responses rather than spontaneous responses.
3. Lying to the patient about one's opinions, attitudes, or feelings.
4. Withholding expressions of like, dislike, boredom, irritation.

Proof, of course, is required to support the hypothesis that an *I-Thou* relationship, marked by unreserve in both parties, is the means and the goal of therapy. But review of existing studies and opinions points to the hypothesis that resistance to authentic being in the therapist is a deterrent to growth of being in the patient.

Another implication of authenticity in the therapist seems to be this: a therapeutic relationship can change the therapist as much as it does the patient. This means that those who wish to leave their being and their growth unchanged should not become therapists.

It would seem that we can propose a hypothesis that could be tested, namely, that spontaneous self-disclosure in a therapist reinforces, or is a condition for, authentic disclosure and growth in the patient, while impersonality, technical behavior, and resistance to being reinforces the like in the patient.* I believe therapists could judge their own protocols for examples of such behavior and then explore relationships between such behavior and the subsequent behavior of the patient.

The question may properly be raised, "What is so good, or therapeutic, about a qualified therapist's spontaneity in his relationships with his patient? Why should it promote growth and wellness in patients, when the spontaneous behavior of the patient's family and friends has not produced these outcomes?" Indeed, the spontaneous responses of the patient's family and friends may have contributed to the development of pathology in the patient.

---

*Leonard Krasner, a brilliant researcher in the operant conditioning of verbal behavior, wrote me thus: ". . . it may very well be that research will indicate that the most effective therapists 'are themselves' in their relationship with the patient. However, I would feel that the therapist acting 'spontaneously' still represents a person who has been highly 'programmed' via his training, schooling, and previous interpersonal contacts. Probably the most effective way to 'control' another person's behavior is to 'be spontaneous' in the relationship with them. Of course, what I am suggesting is that there is no such thing as spontaneity. Anyway, we can probably get into a good controversy on this" (Personal Correspondence, April 11, 1961).

For a full elucidation of Krasner's views, see Krasner, L. The Therapist as a Social Reinforcement Machine. In Strupp,[124] H. H., and Luborsky, L., Research in Psychotherapy, Vol. II, American Psychological Association, Washington, D. C., 1926, pp. 61–94. The recent work of Truax and Carkhuff,[127] confirms this point.

A tentative answer to these questions would seem to be that the therapist, first of all, has a broader and deeper perspective on the dynamics of behavior than laymen would have. Second, he will not be so readily threatened by the patient's pathology or by the patient's growth. Third, the therapist is resolutely committed to promotion of growth and fuller functioning, whereas family and friends of the patient may, without their awareness, be spontaneously reinforcing the patient's pathology and impeding his efforts to grow. Finally, but not least in importance, the setting in which therapy usually is transacted is one which fosters full self-disclosure from the patient and attentive listening in the therapist. To be really heard is a rarity in everyday life.

Another question that arises in this: Is the spontaneity of a trained therapist of a different kind and quality and effect from the spontaneity of family members and that of a beginning therapist who has not yet even become the master of his techniques? My supposition is that the spontaneity that transcends technique is different from beginners' or laymen's spontaneity, different because of the fact that the therapist has been through a disciplined training program. Among other things, the discipline in technique introduces the beginning therapist to a mode of relating to others that is different from the modes he learned as he was socialized; it is a sort of weaning from previously unexamined patterns of interpersonal behavior. *What seems called for in most training programs, however, is encouragement and direction in modes of transcending or abandoning self-conscious or automatized technique in relating to patients.* Many therapists come to feel guilty when their own growth makes their techniques seem restrictive and when they impulsively respond to a patient at a real-self level. Those of us who train psychotherapists have much to learn from Zen masters in the art of eliciting unpremeditated behavior from our well-indoctrinated pupils.

Perhaps these comments about resistance to authentic being in the therapist belong more properly to the later stages of therapy, those that lie beyond what Jung[36] spoke of as the stage of confession. Jung divided the therapeutic process into a stage of confession, a stage of explanation, a stage of education, and finally, a stage of transformation. Possibly technique, such as reflection and interpretation, or even "reinforcement," brings a patient through the stages of confession and explanation, but leaves the therapist untouched and unresponsive as a person. If therapy is to proceed through the stages of education and transformation, resistance to authentic being in the therapist must be overcome, and he must encounter and grow with his patient.

18

The Psychotherapist
As Exemplar

Analogies reveal similarities between things, and conceal differences. Psychotherapists have been likened to physicians, repairmen, thought reformers, animal trainers, and "persuasion" experts concerned with influencing behavior and experience. There is a sense in which the psychotherapeutic task resembles that of guide and mentor, of guru, exemplar, priest or rabbi. This is the perspective from which I want to look at this calling.

I

Psychology and psychotherapy have existed for eighty years as self-conscious professions The world has changed radically since the 1880s—the Victorian age collapsed and ushered in World Wars I,

II, and the iminence of III. Revolutions have occurred in several major nations and dozens of minor ones. Man invaded outer space and rediscovered "inner space." Each of these events has affected man's awareness of his own being, of other men's perspectives, and of the possibilities of the world. Each expansion of man's consciousness has reopened the questions: how to live, how to be, how to pass the time?

Up to the present, psychotherapists have functioned as emergency socialization agents; their job has been to correct the failures of family, school, and other socialization agencies to "shape up" a citizen whose behavior would not be a problem to everyone else. People who didn't "fit" were designated mentally ill. An entire mythology of illness and its cure was gradually evolved by the medical profession, and no psychotherapist was unaffected by this ideology. Psychologists, clergymen, social workers, and counselors of all kinds were trained to view misfitting people as sufferers from "mental disease,"[125] and they were led to believe that if they mastered certain theories and techniques for transacting with *Them*, the patients, they would effect a cure. In this way, *We*, the psychotherapists—solid, conforming professional men with a stake in the status quo—served society, and we could take pride in the fact that we did it well, earning our money with hard, scientifically informed work. We always were pledged to foster and protect our patients' well-being but, curiously enough, our concepts of wellness were well-nigh identical with those versions of personality that fit the social system that subsidized us, with its established class structure and its resistance to change. Revolutionaries, anarchists and rebels against the status quo (including hippies, poets, painters, and writers) could conveniently be seen as sufferers from unresolved Oedipus conflicts. We psychotherapists and investigators did not seriously view each man as a unique source of authentic experience, a perspective that in a more pluralistic, enlightened society might be *confirmed* rather than invalidated. We shared the short-sightedness of our established society, and called the officially sanctioned view of the world "reality-contact" and everything else madness or autism. From this view, people who want to make love, not war, are seen as impractical, schizoid, or seditious. No matter what our private sentiments may have been, we were unwittingly pledged to protect the status quo by invalidating the experience of those who found it unlivable. We called this invalidation "treatment." In effect, we were a peculiar breed of commissars, pledged to alter experiencing that was designated "sick" and to replace it with those modes called "normal." Like it or not: there is a politics of psychotherapy just as there is, in Laing's[65] words, a "politics of experience."

II

Man can experience himself and the world in myriad ways. Being can be likened to a projective test. To insist the world has one meaning rather than another is *politics*. To persuade a man that his experience is not real or worthless is to be a propagandist for some vested interest. We have been confirming what Freud, with incredible courage, found for himself—that our possibilities of experiencing are infinite and infinitely beyond that splinter of awareness we acknowledge, call "normal," and disclose to others. In fact, to the extent that we find our own ordinary consciousnesses banal, we have an answer to a riddle: How was it possible for Freud for so many years to spend twelve to fourteen hours daily listening to people disclose their offbeat experiencing to him without swooning from fatigue or boredom? Users of LSD and marijuana offer the hint of an answer. Freud encouraged people to disclose their unselected experience and I have little doubt that it "turned him on." His psychoanalytic practice must have felt like a forty-year psychedelic trip, or forty years in a gallery of surrealistic art. Hour after hour, day after day, exposed to dreams, fantasies and memories that shattered his conventional rubrics and expectations about the human experience—it couldn't help but expand his awareness of his own being and of the possibilities for experiencing the world. That highly prized state, "being normal," must have looked like banality incarnate to a man who had dauntlessly opened Pandora's box and become privy to the secrets of expanded experiencing, which he found in himself and in those who consulted with him. Each disclosure from a patient must have exploded his concepts and expectations of what is possible.

I think that, in keeping Pandora's box open, we have been infected, or perhaps it is better to say disaffected. We have been infected with the truth that we can experience much more than we permit ourselves, and more than the guardians of the status quo would like us to. And we may have been disaffected from unthinking compliance to the established ways of living our lives, ways of relating to our fellows, ways of experiencing and living in our bodies. We are starting to study man-for-himself—for his possibilities of development and fulfillment that go beyond mere conformity with prevailing norms. And, properly enough, we are starting by studying ourselves.

III

There is no more THEM—only us, seekers after meaning in a social structure that aims to shrink our being, but in a world that requires us to grow. If we insist that patients and subjects belong in the category of THEM, then I, for one, have become one of THEM. I have come to believe that my task, as a psychotherapist, is no longer a specialized paramedical praxis. Rather it is more akin to the mission of an explorer assigned to discover and test ways to relate to others and to the social order that keep one fit, loving, growing, and inventive in the world, ways that evoke new possibilities for achievement, contributions, and enjoyment. My criterion of success in this quest is not solely whether my behavior appears "normal" to others; but, rather my experience of feeling free, responsible, potent, and alive. The criterion of "success" has shifted from exclusive attention to behavior to concern for the quality of experience.

I have been for too long aware that, in appearing normal to others, I felt benumbed and dead within, a habit-ridden plaything of social pressures and expectation. And I have known too many people—fellow seekers (I used to call them patients)—who were exemplary in their conduct, but dead or desperate inside, and who could tolerate their "normal" existence only with the aid of booze or tranquilizers, or periodic hospitalization for an ulcer.

A new specialist is called for in our time, and I believe those of us who presently are psychotherapists may be in the best position to grow beyond our training into the new role. I haven't an acceptable name for this specialist, but I see him as a Westernized version of his Eastern counterpart, the *guru* or teacher. We might call him an existential guide, a "psychedelic man," a consciousness-expanding expert, a growth counselor, or a self-actualization agent. He is a guide to more expanding, fulfilled and fulfilling ways to experience life as a person. He is a "world"* shatterer and rebuilder. As such, he has a robust interest in his own fulfillment, and he pursues this, in part, by helping others to fulfill themselves. But part of his function is as an *examplar* of a turned-on life, a revealer and sharer of how *he* has found his way. He is himself "reborn," in the Sufi sense, or awakened and liberated in the sense of the Zen masters or Taoist teachers. He is a Bodhisatva rather than the Buddha himself—awakened, but not out of this world. He remains in dialogue with those of his fellow seekers who are themselves seeking to become men rather than mystified social functionaries. He shows and tells how he has been awakened, and serves as a guide to others, to help them find their way in their world. He is an experimental existentialist, literally. He experiments with *his* existence, seeking ways that generate maximum enlightenment, freedom, and love.

This view of a psychotherapist as a guru, teacher, or psychedelic man has implicit in it an entire new theory of suffering, growth, practice, settings for practice, schools for training—the total paraphernalia of a profession. But first, it calls for an enlightened perspective on society and for expanded views of human possibility that are authenticated by having discovered new possibilities within oneself. It calls for a "going away" and then for a return, re-

---

*The word "world" is used here to refer to the way in which a person experiences the existence of the world: what he perceives and ignores, how he attaches meaning and value to the world as he experiences it.

newed. It calls for a kind of death and a kind of rebirth. One can easily see adumbrations with Eastern philosophies, Jewish mysticism, early Christian existential (lived) theology, Marxist social criticism and utopianism, current existential phenomenology, and Freud's work, in this perspective. Ancient myths about leaving home to live and learn, then coming back to establish dominion over one's kingdom are also relevant. From this standpoint, hippies and "drop-outs" have taken just the first step, the leaving. If they are men (and women), they will return to renew and humanize the society they left.

IV

I took part in a symposium at the Southeastern Psychological Association on "Innovations In Psychotherapy." I spoke of innovations in a *psychotherapist*—myself. I spoke of what I have done with and beyond the training I received to become a psychotherapist. I spoke of the books I had read; of impasses in my therapeutic work and personal growth, and how I transcended them or failed to. I spoke of the impact on my work as a therapist produced by my experience as husband and father, colleague of others, teacher of students; of the influence of my research in self-disclosure and body-experience, and my experience as one of THEM (the patients) on my work as psychotherapist. I noted that we tend to limit our dialogue at professional meetings to ways in which we have succeeded in helping Them by trying out psychoanalytic techniques, Rogerian techniques, Perls[91] techniques —but we have not deliberately acknowledged one another as *persons*, nor have we shared our problems and solutions in staying alive and growing. We have not deliberately explored or reflected upon the ways in which we behaved ourselves into sickness and out of it. Our "technologies" remain authorized ways to practice upon Them that, in principle, anyone can learn.

As for myself, I have found in my meetings with people who consult me that WE enter into dialogue, and my commitment is to help the other become more enlightened, more liberated from the bondage of habit, social pressure, the past, of some one mode of experiencing. I try to awaken the seeker to the plastic possibilities that inhere in his "facticity." I try to help him reinvent himself and his situation, and then help him try to fulfill the invention. To implement this project, I respond in any way and every way that is available to me in the context of dialogue. My commitment in the dialogue is not to a theory, technique, or setting, but to the project of abetting another person's wholeness and growth. Of necessity, there are technical ways of embodying this project, but these always reach an impasse, and at the impasse, the seriousness of my commitment receives its test: Am I committed to my theory and techniques or to the project? In the context of dialogue I don't hesitate to share any of my experience with existential binds roughly comparable to those in which the seeker finds himself (this is now called "modelling"); nor do I hesitate to disclose my experience of him, myself, and our relationship as it unfolds from moment to moment. Nor do I hesitate, when it becomes relevant, to tell a joke, give a lecture for a few minutes on my view of how he is being mystified by others in his life and how he is mystifying others. I might give Freudian or other types of interpretations. I might teach him such Yoga know-how or tricks for expanding body-awareness as I have mastered or engage in arm wrestling or hold hands or hug him, if that is the response that emerges in the dialogue. I encourage him to try experiments with his own existence, like trying the risky business of authenticity, or changing living arrangements.

Our relationship begins almost always with the seeker expecting it to unfold in a technically predictable and prescribed way (as outlined in popular books, TV, and movies). In fact, I feel pressure from him to stay in an impersonal and technical role. I respect this, but respond with the invitation to dialogue. If he accepts the invitation—and gradually he does—the relationship becomes a shared quest for authentic ways he might live that generate wholeness and growth. I do not hesitate to play a game of handball with a seeker or visit him in his home—if this unfolds in the dialogue. The technical ways of behaving we have called "psychotherapeutic intervention" may have functioned as authentic paths to enlightenment and liberation for someone, at some time. But to congeal them as orthodoxies is to meet a seeker's "hang-ups" with "hang-ups" engendered in an academy. Technical approaches limit the therapist's capacity for relevant response in dialogue and they confuse commitments. *A therapist is defined by his project, not his means.*

The paradox I am discovering is that the most efficient means of fostering therapeutic aims is by sharing the fruits of my quest for fuller life (about which I am ultimately serious) with the seeker. This liberates me from technical rigidities. I experience myself as an explorer of ways I invent, or that others invent and I learn about and try, to make life more meaningful for me, and I then share, show, and co-experience these ways with the seeker.

I don't think one can be trained to become this kind of psychotherapist-cum-guru-cum-teacher. It is rather a case of allowing oneself, first, to be trained into one ideology and praxis, then to allow growing experience to shatter or challenge it in a dialectical moment of antithesis—and then to transcend the contradictions in a synthesis that becomes possible through a new commitment to more comprehensive goals This is what Yoga and Zen are about—they are ways of shattering training, of bringing a person back to center, before commitments, so that he can draw upon more of his possibilities in new commitments. Dialogue is a Yoga of interpersonal relationships

I think that it is time now for a therapist to tell those who consult with him whether he is a commissar, a trainer to the status quo, or a responsible liberator from congealed experience and the rigid, sickening behavior it mediates. Perhaps there will be joint practices, where Dr. John specializes in helping socially inept, neurotic, and psychotic people (if we still use such dehumanizing jargon) manage acceptable social behavior. He will help the Incomplete Square to become boxed in or bagged. Then Dr. Bill may take over, to liberate and awaken the seeker to more of his possibilities beyond those he has attained.

Perhaps, too, hospitals will be visited only by people who need a fracture mended or a wound stanched. The community mega-hospitals can then be replaced by places where people can go *before* they sicken—when they notice the early signs that their life style is sickening them—and where they can learn and be shown that experience and air outside our conventional rubrics can invigorate and renew. Psychotherapists and counselors have a prime opportunity to take those first exciting glimpses and those first bracing breaths

19

Self-Disclosure And The Encounter Group Leader

Gimmicks, gadgets, and techniques are the genius of America. What have these to do with a person's growth, which *happens* as he struggles to reinvent his world, encountering obstacles and helpers along the way. Are encounter groups "gimmicks and techniques"?

I first heard about "encounter groups" as something special when I went to Esalen Institute, shortly after returning from a year in England. I was to conduct an informal seminar advertised, ambiguously enough, as "A Weekend With Sidney Jourard," to discuss *The Transparent Self* and anything else I was up to. About 150 people jammed into the meeting room at the main lodge of Esalen, and I began to talk about self-disclosure, thinking that was appropriate. Every few minutes someone would interrupt my brilliant oratory and say something like, "But Dr. Jourard (or Sid), you've written about self-disclosure in *The Transparent Self*, and you're not telling us anything about you. Disclose yourself to us!" I ignored several of these comments, but one person (I forget whether man or woman) was persistent. I said "Damn it! You're not asking for self-disclosure, which I'm doing! You seem to want a strip-tease! Would you like me to undress?" I continued, "Look, if you want to sit with me, and really talk, I'm ready. But I'm a private person. Respect this as much as I respect your right to disclose or withhold." This was a brief encounter between the other and me, and an invitation to continuing encounter which the other person declined. Esalen Institute, I learned, was a place where many "encounter groups" were conducted.

I knew about group dynamics and sensitivity training, and I had gotten some training in group therapy. But as my research in self-disclosure progressed, I came to think of individual and group therapy not so much as "treatment" as an invitation to authentic disclosure and self-reinvention. For four years, I had conducted what the dean called "Faculty Training Group" with my colleagues in a college of nursing. I thought of it as a "disclosure group"; the nursing faculty seemed to view it as a therapy group. My aim was to invite the nursing instructors to be less bitchy, defensive, game-playing one-up-women, hoping they would then serve as more human and humane role models for their students. I think I succeeded to a modest extent. And I learned something about the way training in professions dehumanizes young practitioners. (See Chapters 20-22)

I have been conducting something like "encounter groups" since 1965, and I had been "in" them (through my association with the American Academy of Psychotherapists) before that date. My feelings about the "encounter group phenomenon" are mixed. I'm delighted that people have begun to gather in small groups to try really to address one another in the spirit of goodwill. It's reminiscent of the early Christian church. And I am somewhat suspicious about the growing technology of "group process," and encounter groups that are "led." There are manuals for group leaders available, giving opening gambits, nonverbal games, touching exercises, group gropes and the like—like rainy-day suggestions, the boon for all who direct summer camps for children. I have created one or two such games myself, and intend to develop more. But everything depends on the projects, the purposes for which people enter into or lead an encounter group. I run them, when asked, with the aim of encouraging personal growth in myself and the others through encounter with one's situation and the other people in it. And I invite encounter in my individual counseling, my teaching, and my personal life, for the same reason.

What are personal growth, one's situation, and encounter? I have grown when I perceive the changes that occur in my embodied self and my world—my situation—decide how I next want to be in this world and how I want the world to be for me, and then act. Change in my world happens continuously as process— the result of agency other than my own. And change is consequent upon praxis, that is my own acts, acts which affect the world as well as me, the actor. I discover change when I pause from my projects and take a fresh look at me and my world. And change discloses itself to me in moments of surprise, when I find that the people and things are not as I believed. At these moments my situation becomes a question, an invitation and a challenge. The question: "What is my situation? Do I want it to endure?" Whether my answer is yes or no, my situation challenges me to act, to preserve it or let it drift as it will. If I choose to change it, then I must envision, however dimly, a better situation for me, a better way for me to be (and be seen) in the world. And I must envision a better way for the world to be for me. Given the image, I must then act, to "actualize" it.

My situation is "factical." It is the facts of my condition and the condition of my world that are disclosed to me when I survey my situation. It is man's lot in this world to acknowledge the change of the world and himself, change which follows the "process" of the world and change which follows his own acts. And it is every man's lot to face the changed situation—change that has occurred behind his dim perception of the world until he peers through the veil—and answer the question, "What will I do in, with, and to this changed situation that I confront, the situation which encounters me?" Without such true perception and challenge in a situation, there is no encounter, and there is no growth. And if you are part of my situation and I part of yours, there can be no encounter and no growth unless we disclose ourselves to each other in truth. Then I encounter you, and you encounter me. Our worlds merge into a shared realm of "between."

The difference between my encounter with some nonhuman part of my world and an encounter between you and me is this: I encounter a tree when I perceive it as it now is. The tree does not know it is perceived. When you and I disclose ourselves to one another in dialogue, I perceive you and am perceived in return; and I know that you perceive me, and you know I perceive you, because I tell you what of you I perceive. We both have the chance to grow through our encounter, if we dare be and disclose who we are just then. Because that is our ground, our situation.

I do not encounter my situation. I can only offer encounter, and that only to another person. Encounter *happens* to me when I let my situation speak to me, touch me, blast my preconceptions and let me know what is there. Because what is there is not what I assumed, presumed, or imagined. The encounter is fulfilled when I acknowledge my situation, and respond with the truth of my being—which includes my vision of a better situation.

My situation and yours are complex. Mine includes what I perceive and misperceive of my body and the world beyond my body through my several sensory systems ("receivers" of the disclosure of the world). And it includes my recollections and feelings and imaginings and fantasies and thoughts, as these exist for me right now. In fact, my memories, thoughts and imaginings "turn off" my perception, so that I no longer receive the disclosures transmitted by my body and the world. To think, imagine, or remember with full attentiveness is to be functionally blind, deaf, anesthesic, shut off from the world. When I am "in my head," I am out of my situation, and I do not perceive it as it is. I cannot change my situation until I know it, let it encounter me in the intense immediacy of perception.

Everyone is a specialist at some kind of "blindness." This person cannot see, that one cannot smell, the other has not felt, tasted, or heard what his situation is saying. Everyone's perceptual grasp of his situation is partial. If a group of people share a situation, each can disclose his perspective to the others, thus inviting them to see, hear, or smell and feel what he does, but which they do not; but they can. Thus, the shared disclosures of how it is with me that a group-for-encounter affords can turn a person's perception on and enlarge his awareness of his situation. If people likewise share their memories, inventiveness, and ways of construing situations, they likewise grant an invitation to others to experience in comparable ways. And if they show one another how they cope, they afford the others an opportunity to copy or adapt these ways for themselves. My disclosure in words and actions is thus a precious gift to those who receive it. When I am in your situation, and let myself be perceived, I have truly helped you to awaken and grow.

But I have met (or, better, not encountered) numerous people —whom I think of as "T-group bums," or encounter group bloodhounds—who can enter a town or neighborhood, sniff the air, and say, "There's an encounter group going on somewhere," and they track it down. Once in, they cry, swear, touch, insist people stop the bullshit intellectualizing and get down to the nitty gritty, the gut level, here-and-now, and then go home with pleasant memories, and a routine, cosmetic existence. There is nothing wrong with following the groups, and developing expertise, comparing Schutz[111] with Perls[91] with Rogers etc. Fun is hard to find, and I'm all for it wherever it can happen. Moreover, watching a master do his thing in a group is a much less bloody spectator sport than boxing. And there are the equivalent of fan clubs developing. "I like the way Schutz handles body contact better than Bindrim does," one buff might say to another.

Encounter groups at their best can be places to go to play and to grow. I see groups in which I take part as an opportunity to present to those attending who I am, where I am in any spheres of my life I feel comfortable talking about, how I struggle against the barriers that get in the way of my projects and my growth. Someone present always reacts to me, and we are off! Where we go from there, and what happens for the next hours or days depends on all of us. I don't take responsibility for everyone participating, everyone having a good time, everyone touching somebody or being touched, though at a given moment I may ask someone to join me in a headstand or a dance. The only thing I really try for, while I am in a group where encounter may happen, is to be *available*, in touch with my own state of being. And to disclose my state of being, my feelings, wishes, fantasies, my action whenever it is relevant in a dialogue between myself and whoever I am personally *with* just then. At the time I am in dialogue with another, everyone else is part of the background, spectators. Whenever two others have commenced to encounter one another, letting dialogue unfold in words, feelings, and actions, I become part of the audience, and sometimes I will tell others who try to interfere to leave the two alone. But I always hope that the pair who are "at it" will themselves ask the intruder to stay out or invite him into an effort at a triad.

I am anxious at the start of every group meeting because I have no plan, no routine, and I intend for it always to be that way for me. I do not practice techniques of "good group leading," because that implies trying to "have it made," to be a competent practitioner of someone's techniques that are appropriate for Us to practice on Them. I don't believe in Them. "Them," "him," or "her" are ways for me to experience a You, who properly is one of Us. When I am in a group-for-encounter and find I am thinking about you others as Them, I immediately speak out and say, "I'm out of this scene right now. I wonder why?" But I also feel free to leave the group scene, either by getting up and walking out for awhile or by retreating into my own experience, to think, to tune in on myself. And if someone intrudes, I say, "You are intruding just now. I'd like to sit here in silence for awhile."

If someone in the group talks to me about somebody else in

the group, I invite him to speak directly to the one he is discussing, so that encountering might happen. I don't know how to make encounter come into being. I can only be open and ready for it to happen and committed to respond in honest spontaneity to the one with whom I have engaged.

I am vulnerable to Berne-ish games,[6] to being conned and manipulated, until I discover that that is what is going on. Then I tell what my experience is, and withdraw from the game, unless it is fun. I don't take pride in being expert at interpreting games, transference phenomena, defenses, etc., though I am pretty good at it when it seems meaningful to pull back and be a critical diagnostician.

I inevitably find in leading a group-for-encounter that someone present is trying to write my autobiography. When I appear different from what they expected, they become angry or disappointed, and try to invite me to be the one they imagine I am. I decline the invitation. But often I awaken to myself and find that for the last few minutes I was being someone else, not myself. And I go back to being me and tell what had happened.

I usually decline others' invitations to invent myself to their design. I feel pretty good about myself, in spite of assorted hang-ups, inconsistencies, and the like. I don't hesitate, however, to disclose my view of how the other person might be. I encourage him to reinvent himself and his world in any way that makes sense to him.

This gives me an opportunity in the group (as well as in these pages) to expound my view of the human situation. I am a psychologist, and I see part of my job as that of forming an image, or "model" of man in his situation that makes man intelligible, but which does not warp or diminish him to fit the image. I'm not satisfied with conceptual models which regard man as an analogue of a rat, pigeon, monkey or computer—though much of what we learn about those beings does throw some light on how you and I function. I am a "humanistic," not an animalistic or mechanistic, psychologist. I am committed to a view of man as a person—a being like me. And like you, when I experience you as a person. So I believe that anything I learn about me is your possibility, as your way is mine. When you trust me enough to let me experience you, your "insides" as well as your behavioral shell, you are augmenting this emerging image or theory of man as possible person in possible worlds. The best analogues I can think of for man is *artist* and mimic. Man is like the parrot—he has no native song, no God-given essence that he unfolds like a tape. He has to copy or invent, his speech and his being. Here I agree with Rank in the choice of conceptual models. But not in terminology, necessarily.

One of my projects, then, is seeing how far I can rewrite psychology in the light of an image of man as artist and mimic, as opposed to man as organism, as animal, or as machine. A mimic, after all, is an artist of a sort. I see no contradiction among research, practice, teaching, and writing when I proceed from the assumption that every man, woman, and child is more like me and you than he is like a machine or animal and that we are all artists. I don't have a special "researcher" self, a "therapist" self, a "teacher" self, and a "personal" self. These are names for places to do my thing.

I view the world as plastic; not synthetic plastic, but plastic like plasticene. Everything has its "plasticity quotient"—its amenability to change before it is destroyed or transformed into something else. I am my world, and I can change it in many particulars without destroying it or me. Everything has its plasticity quotient, whether it be my appearance, my behavior, my relationships with others, the landscape, the arrangement of furniture in my room, the behavior of others in my world. Each moment of existence is an invitation or challenge to me to let the arrangement of my situation be as it now is or to change it, reinvent it, or invite it to change. Every project of mine projects an image of a possible me in a possible world in my imaginative consciousness. My action is the work of a skilled or unskilled artist-craftsman, aimed at transmuting the image into actuality. Most often, I invent and reinvent me and my situation according to the same template, day after day, year after year. That's why I say I am an artist manqué.

It's not necessary radically to change one's personal world daily. But sometimes the situation in which a person finds himself—including his way of being in that situation—is unlivable. The other people in it may be inviting him to die, or to live in ways that are sickening him, though these ways are pleasing to the others; and he has accepted their invitations. He may view himself and his world as unchangeable and grit his teeth enduring daily existence with no hope of escape.

If you regard yourself as unchangeable, as the victim of your past and your heredity, I respect this as your view, but I disagree with it. My view of you is more scientifically informed—you and your situation embody incredible possibilities for change. So I don't hesitate to confront you with my view of your possibilities. If I say, "You can change your way of being," you may reply, "I cannot." I regard your statement not as a matter of scientific fact, but as a stubbornly held commitment to keep your situation the same. You and I may then argue. If you win the argument, you lose much of your life. If you lose the argument, you win. I used to call this argument "psychotherapy," whether it went on in my consulting room or in the encounter group setting.

In a group-for-encounter, I assume that spontaneous encounter is a good thing, that when it happens, people's views of themselves and the other are challenged, up-ended, and that they attain a larger perspective on their own worlds. With an enlarged view of an enlarged world, there is more room for them to move, change, and grow. And so I invite people to encounter me, or anyone else, in the spontaneous flow of group interaction.

But if I am charged with "leading" the group, I take certain responsibilities. I assign ground rules—no "ganging up" on anyone, however hung-up he is on some way of being, so he will then conform to some emerging group norm. That is brainwashing, not encounter, and I oppose it. In encounter, both parties are changed. I am committed to a view of society and our group as a place where eccentricity, one's own pace, and one's privacy all are respected. I "lead" by example. I don't cast myself into the role of facilitator, interpreter of group process, or interpreter of psychodynamics. Not in an encounter group. I participate with, and risk, as much of myself as I have freely available. I may lecture for awhile, tell a joke, or tell someone who asks me what I think of him. I may ask him to tell me (and the group) about his situation at home and explore with him ways in which he might commence the project of reinventing his world.

If someone complains that I and another, or some other pair monopolize the time, I invite him to dive in, participate more fully, or shout. The time "up front" is available to all, usually in pairs, but sometimes three, four, or five people will get some honest interchange going.

I view encounter as more than exchanging words. Hugging, holding, occasionally wrestling, shouting, dancing, showing off— whatever is someone's "thing" just then may happen, and I or the others reply in ways that express our being. At least I do. The purpose in all this is to afford myself and the others the chance to discover and live more of ourselves than we usually do "back home" and to shatter our concepts of ourselves, our situations, and each other. But I am keenly aware that the aim is not just to "have" an experience in the group which, at home, becomes a happy or frightening memory; it is to encourage a person to be and to disclose more of his possibilities here and back home. I see my groups as settings for the experience of authentic being-with-others, and as places to begin the project of reinventing one-self and one's situations wherever one is—so one can be free to live, move, and grow.

Though I participate in encounter groups somewhat as I've described, I always feel a certain artificiality prevails. My most common experiences is with weekend encounter groups, or work-shops, at various "growth centers." I don't see any magic in these "happenings," though sometimes a participant or I will undergo a realization, a confirmation, or a challenge that carries over back home. I like best to be with people who have committed them-selves to a continuous project of growth and self-renewal and who share with each other their ways of overcoming obstacles, because we can begin being artists of our situations by copying one another —if we show, and show off ourselves to one another.

If I or the other participants leave the group experience with a heightened and confirmed sense of our identity and the recollection of some intense and meaningful encounters with others and with our courage and imaginations enlivened, I count it a "successful" group. I am suspicious of sudden conversions, and more impressed by quiet resolve to change one's world so it is more fit for an eccentric human like you or me to live in.

I have no systematic follow-up of the persons who have been in groups with me. Some have written me of changes they began in the group and which they resolutely carried over into the rest of their lives. I have not heard from persons for whom the weekend, series of meetings, or the "marathon" might have been unrewarding. We need more data on this.

I see groups-for-encounter as places and times for each who is present to disclose himself as he now is and for each to respond, truly respond, to what has thus been revealed. In such interplay, encounter might happen, someone may experience himself as truly addressed, or truly answered. Sometimes I feel truly asked to be a teacher or discloser of something I know or am. It is at these times that I may invite one other, or several others, or all in the group to play a game for the experience that it may afford them. One game is the "dialogue game." I list a number of topics on a blackboard,* or ask people to write them down on a slip of paper: "my favorite foods," "my hobbies," "my work," "my past life with my family," "my marriage," etc. I pair the people at random and ask them to take turns disclosing themselves to their partner on each topic. The only rules for the game are to speak truth; to respect one's own and the other's reluctance or embar-

---

*The research questionnaire shown on pp. 213–216 can be used by anyone as a source of topics for the game. Indeed, some of my students have typed the topics on 3 x 5 cards, and used the cards as tokens in a game of spiritual "strip-poker." The winner of the hand asks the losers to disclose the information on their cards.

rassment; and to let it be known when one does not wish to disclose. Players of the game often find that, under the protective mantle of being "told" to disclose themselves, they commence a dialogue that lasts up to eight hours, or a lifetime. When the "players" are done, we reconvene as a group, and often find that disclosure within the group is less reserved, as if the game has enabled the players to take off masks and armor. But just as important to me as a teacher is to give the players a chance to discover their limits to dialogue—threat, embarrassment—to respect these and to explore their possibilities of gently pressing against them toward fuller unreserve with a partner. Sometimes, instead of a disclosure game, I will suggest a physical contact game where partners will, in full respect for their own and their partner's feelings, give a back rub, a foot rub, a belly rub, a buttocks rub, and, moreover, do this in silence.* Again, the aim is as much for each person to discover his embarrassment or shyness and to disclose this, as it is to enable physical contact to happen. Such games, or experiments, are intended as didactic experiences as well as ways for inviting encounter between the players.

Often, in a group, members will begin to talk of their weaknesses, hang-ups, problems, peccadilloes and the like. I find that such "confessing" is harmless if it helps the people present to realize that everyone has this dimension to his existence. But I don't hesitate to disclose my own excellences, to show off, as an invitation and challenge to the others to explore and to demonstrate what is magnificent about themselves. In fact, group members may help a person recognize some realms of magnificence which he never acknowledged before, but which we all have as our possibilities, buried under habit, faint-heartedness, and lack of imagination or insight.

There are many ways for a person to be. I see myself as engaged in this world, trying with no guarantee of success to make it fit for me to live and grow in. I cannot pursue this goal for long if I am chronically unguarded, because I may be hurt. I will not

*This game as well can be played with dice or with cards—the winner receiving a careful massage on the body parts he has staked.

move far if I am chronically cunning or armored. Nor will I get anywhere without courage, resolve, and, above all, inventiveness. This is the "self" with which I "lead" the other persons in groups I conduct. I lead, if at all, by showing, or showing off. There is nothing, that is, no *thing* to show. Just a way of being, and being-with, here. I can enter your world, as one who invites your growth or as a strangler of your possibilities, a prophet of stasis. I try to be the former.

PART 6

A HUMAN WAY OF BEING FOR NURSES (AND OTHER HELPING PROFESSIONALS)

An Introduction

The next three chapters were written expressly for nurses, but with a bit of imagination on the reader's part, they can be read with profit by physicians, teachers, clergymen, dentists, lawyers, counselors and psychotherapists—anyone who is working in a "helping" profession.

There are technical aspects to every helping profession, and these can be mastered by anyone with the wit and endurance to undergo training. Once the basic theories and techniques of a helping profession have been mastered, the beginning practitioner is ready to be turned loose to practice. The question that has long fascinated me is, How, and in what respects, does a professional "helper" grow?

My hypothesis has been that growth beyond technical expertise is *growth as a person among persons—a rehumanizing process.* Many physicians, nurses, psychologists, and teachers remain the same person at age fifty that they were at age fifteen; a little fatter, with graying hair, but no more awakened, enlightened, or accepting of human possibilities. I invite readers who are not nurses to read the next three chapters, and replace the word "nurse" with "physician," "teacher," "counselor," or whatever term describes their own profession.

I believe that professional training encourages graduates to wear a professional mask, to limit their behavior to the range that proclaims their professional status. Thus, nurses are supposed to look and sound like nurses, doctors like doctors, as well as do the work delegated to persons in those roles. Patients are exposed not to *human beings* who have expertise, but to "experts" who are dehumanized and dehumanizing. To spend time in the company of those who will not relate at a human level cannot be health-engendering, either for the patient, or the professional. The next chapters explore the problem of rehumanizing the dehumanized members of the helping professions.

20

The "Manners" Of Helpers And Healers: The Bedside Manner Of Nurses

Many workers in the healing professions assume a "professional manner" as soon as they are in the presence of their clients or patients. Physicians assume a manner of cameraderie, self-assurance, and omniscience "to give the patient confidence." Many psychotherapists grow beards and smoke cigars in imitation of Freud and respond in predictable ways to their patients.

These predictable ways of behaving are often offensive to the victims before whom they are performed. I want to talk about the "bedside manner" of nurses as a peculiar kind of inauthentic behavior that I believe does more harm than good.

Some nurses always smile, others hum, and still others answer all patients' questions about medication with the automatic phrase,

"This will make you feel better." The "bedside manner" appears to be something which the nurse puts on when she dons her uniform. The performance sometimes functions as an emetic for perceptive patients.

As an observer in a hospital situation, I recently noticed some instances of the bedside manner which led me to wonder about the function of this particular pattern of interpersonal behavior. For example, I was in a patient's room interviewing him informally about his background and current preoccupations, and on several occasions nurses entered the room to perform "nursing functions." This man was seriously ill and had much on his mind, but his nurses came in talking cheerfully and did not cease the cheerful discourse until they had left. I had little doubt that the nurses knew no more about this man after they left than they knew when they entered. I verified this guess when I later asked the nurses to tell me about Mr. Jones. One nurse replied, "Oh, he's a nice fellow." The other told me, "He's O.K., though sometimes he's a bit difficult." I asked both of them if they had any idea of what Mr. Jones had on his mind, and each said that so far as she knew, he was cheerful most of the time.

It became apparent that these nurses, who after all are not atypical, had solved the "human relations problem" in nursing by means of stereotyped modes of behavior. Now I would like to discuss the bedside manner in the light of more recent formulations of interpersonal behavior—its origins, functions, and connections with nursing care.

Interpersonal behavior patterns are acquired as means for satisfying needs and for reducing anxiety. Rigid interpersonal behavior has been called "character armor" by one psychotherapist.[95] It serves the function of stifling spontaneity in the person and protecting him from possible hurt coming from the outside. Character armor serves effectively to hide a person's real self, both from himself and from others. Character armor is acquired in situations marked by anxiety, and it protects a person from recurrences of anxiety—and from guilt-provoking impulses and actions.

Doubtless, the bedside manner warrants being regarded as an

instance of character armor, since it is a case of rigid interpersonal behavior. It is acquired as a means of coping with the anxieties engendered by repeated encounters with suffering, demanding patients. If the "armor" is effective, it permits the nurse to go about her duties unaffected by any disturbing feelings of pity, anger, inadequacy, or insecurity. It is as if the nurse, early in training, asked the question, "How should I behave in the presence of patients?" By trial and error, or perhaps through emulation of a highly esteemed instructor, she arrives at a formula which "works." Hence, one nurse might habitually crack jokes, another might look and act hurried, and still another might mother all her patients on the premise that all patients are babies.

But let us look more closely at these stereotyped interpersonal behavior patterns to see some consequences to which they lead. We know that one person's behavior toward another is a controlling factor in the behavior of the other person. Thus, maternal behavior tends to pull dependent behavior from the other person. Joking behavior tends to evoke joking behavior in return from the other.[69] People seem to function most comfortably with others when the latter limit their reactions to some fixed range. Some people are unable to cope with another's tears, some cannot handle another's anger, some cannot deal with another's sexuality, and still others cannot tolerate spontaneous expressions of despair. Unwittingly, they behave in the presence of others so that the others will find it difficult to express these threatening patterns of behavior. We may assume, then, that one of the latent functions of the bedside manner is to reduce the probability that patients will behave in ways that are likely to threaten the professional person.

There is, however, a consequence of rigid interpersonal behavior which can gravely interfere with the avowed aims of the healing professions. Healers are dedicated to cooperation with the forces that abet recovery from illness. Doctors and nurses traditionally pursue these professional aims through such means as administering medications, providing physical care, and ensuring that standards of hygiene and physical comfort are maintained while the patient is in their care. No self-respecting nurse or doctor would overlook such vital information as the patient's temperature, blood pressure, and other physical signs of progress or regress with respect to recovery. Yet, *the bedside manner is nicely designed to exclude a highly important source of information that has much pertinence to the optimum response of the patient to treatment. I have reference here to information which can only be obtained through the patient's verbal disclosure of what is on his mind.* Just as thermometers and sphygmomanometers reveal something about the state of the patient's body—which nurses and physicians are concerned with—so does verbal self-disclosure reveal something about the state of the patient as a whole person. If the patient has something on his mind, it is possible, even likely, that this "something" may have direct pertinence to his overall problem in health. Thus, he may be gravely worried, or he may have serious misconceptions about his illness, or he may know that he is markedly sensitive to penicillin. I know of several instances of people who nearly died because every time they tried to tell their nurse of their intolerance of penicillin the nurse replied, cheerfully and firmly, as she neatly performed the injection, "The doctor knows what's best; this will help you get well." Nobody listened.

We may propose, then, that *another latent function of the bedside manner is to prevent a patient from disclosing himself, to prevent patients from making themselves known to their nurses and physicians.* Rigid interpersonal behavior presumes that all people before whom it is enacted are alike in personality; to some extent, rigid interpersonal behavior actually provokes a certain uniformity in the behavior of others. But we know that, in spite of certain fundamental human similarities among people, they differ markedly one from the other. It is apparent, then that the *bedside manner seeks to obliterate or to deny individuality in patients;* it unconsciously attempts to enforce a certain uniformity in patients' personalities, the kind of uniformity with which the nurse feels most competent to cope. It seems to be difficult for professional healers to accept the fact that they cannot know any other person —patient, student, friend, or family member—*until they have taken steps to find out who and how he is.*

One important concept, or precept, stemming from the experience of psychotherapists is as follows: "It is important to know the other person's 'self,' that is, how he is experiencing the world." It is important to know the other person's self because his behavior, and even his physiology, is affected by his "phenomenal field." Workers, such as nurses and physicians, who are committed to changing physiology from the pathological range to the healthy range, are obliged to learn as much about a given person as is pertinent to their aims. If they overlook information available only through patient's full disclosure of self, then they are hamstringing their diagnostic and therapeutic endeavors.

Let it be granted, then, that knowledge about a patient's "self" is of value for medical and nursing care. But we have already shown that a stereotyped pattern of interpersonal behavior enacted by many nurses—the bedside manner—is nicely designed to prevent patients from disclosing themselves. *It becomes apparent, then, that the bedside manner can actually obstruct* (or at the very least not help) *attempts to "integrate psychiatric and mental health concepts into programs of nursing education and nursing care."*

Another concept, or principle, which stems from the broad field of mental health maintains that authenticity is an aspect of healthy personality. Neurotic people, and people with "socially patterned defects," which Fromm[34] and Horney[45] described so aptly, are all persons who display varying degrees of "self-alienation." Concretely, this means that they have repressed or suppressed much of their own real and spontaneous reactions to experience. They replace their spontaneous behavior with carefully censored behavior which conforms to a rigid role definition or a rigid and highly limited self-concept. They behave as they "should" behave and feel what they "should" feel. When roles and/or self-concepts exclude too much "real self," a person soon experiences certain symptoms, viz., vague anxiety, depression, and boredom, and if the person has come to neglect the needs and feelings of his body, then such physical symptoms as unwarranted fatigue, headache, and digestive upsets will arise. In short failure or inability to know and be one's real self can make one sick. In extreme cases, where the real self has been well-nigh strangulated, it may happen that there is a "breakthrough," and the person suffers a "nervous breakdown."

People squelch their real selves because they have learned to fear the consequences of authentic being. I have observed that the nurse's bedside manner is not a faithful portrayal of her real self. Is it possible that the role of nurse, as this has been learned during training and in practice, is one which is detrimental to the physical and mental health of nurses? Is it possible that nurses, by attempting to root out their own spontaneity and replace it with stereotyped modes of interpersonal behavior, are actually doing violence to their own personalities and bodies? We may propose that *another latent function of the bedside manner is to foster increasing self-alienation in nurses, thus jeopardizing their own health and well-being.*

There is a connection between a nurse's inability or fear to be her real self while on duty and the blocking of patients' self-disclosure. Research and clinical practice show that one of the factors which promotes honest self-disclosure in a person is an empathic acknowledgment of what has been expressed. Now, if a nurse is afraid and even ignorant of her own self, she is highly likely to be threatened by a patients' real-self expressions. Hence, a patient might send out a "trial balloon" concerning what really is on his mind, only to encounter a response from the nurse which effectively squelches him. A nurse who is more aware of the breadth and depth of her own real self is in a much better position to "empathize" with her patients and to encourage (or at least not block) their self-disclosure. The bedside manner, then, can blind a nurse to much of her own real self; the consequent reduction in insight then impairs empathy with patients. Empathy— the ability to guess what a patient is experiencing in a given situation—is an outgrowth of insight, or self-awareness. *The bedside manner desensitizes a nurse to her own experience and handicaps her attempts to know her patient.*

We have pointed out that the bedside manner was originally

acquired as a kind of protection for the nurse: it kept her relations with patients impersonal and protected her both against becoming known by patients and also against any feelings she might have for patients which she believed she should not have. Suppose one could "strip" a nurse of her bedside manner, just as one could divest her of her uniform? If a person is proud of his or her body's appearance, nakedness will not be much of a threat. If a person is not ashamed of his real self, then disclosure of self should not be highly threatening either. But there is a paradox noticeable in the training of nurses. Beginning students, both in colleges of nursing and in hospital schools of nursing, begin their careers loaded with responsiveness—real-self responsiveness—to the experiences which confront them. They experience and sometimes express feelings of panic, disgust at excreta, shame at exposures of the human body—the gamut of reactions which one might expect from naïve late adolescents. They compare their own feelings and reactions with the examples provided them by their teachers and preceptors and find themselves "inferior." They may even be directly told, "Nurses don't feel like that." Now, in time many of the initial emotional reactions undergone by beginning students will change. The initial shyness in the presence of another's nakedness may change to frank acceptance of nudity. As the girl matures and has more experience with a broader range of human reactions (her own and those of others), her emotional responses to giving injections or enemas may change radically from what they were early in training. But this authentic change will not occur unless the student nurse has been able to acknowledge and express her feelings openly and test all of her expectations with regard to the provoking experiences. If the student has been obliged to deny to her instructors and to herself that she has certain feelings, then she may eventually become ashamed and afraid of her real self. Consequently, she suppresses and represses her honest reactions and replaces them insofar as she is able with what she believes she "should" feel. In time, following the role models available to her, she becomes a nurse with a squelched real self and a contrived bedside manner. It seems likely that the bedside manner which we have been commenting upon is a direct outgrowth of the instructional period in school or college and the apprenticeship period when the student is watching how experienced nurses carry out their work. Stated another way, it seems very likely that students actively learn and are actively taught to be estranged from their real selves—more estranged than their family roles required them to be—and so it is no accident that they arrive at graduation with a cool (or contrivedly warm) bedside manner.

What alternative is available for nurses to take the place of a bedside manner which seems to defeat many of the aims of the nursing profession? How can nurses with a confirmed bedside manner get rid of it, and how can students be trained so that they will not have chronic need to hide their real selves behind a professional mask? Observation has shown that experienced nurses who have been fortunate enough, following a "nervous breakdown," to undergo intensive psychotherapy will abandon their prior rigid interpersonal patterns with patients, displaying greater insight into themselves and greater empathy with their patients. They feel and act more freely with their patients and elicit more self-disclosure from patients. This would imply that all nurses should undergo psychotherapy. In fact, this is impracticable, and it is not certain that it would accomplish its aim. There is growing evidence to show, however, that the average nurse can increase her ability both to promote self-disclosure in patients and to utilize the disclosures as guides for more personalized, "tailor-made" nursing actions. The most direct and simple step which she can take in this direction is to make use of all available time, whether it be ten seconds or half an hour, to permit the patient to talk about what is on his mind. This does not mean formal interviewing. Rather, it implies simply taking steps to become acquainted with this very person to whom one is giving an injection or back rub. It will come as a surprise to many nurses to discover the extent to which they have actually avoided many opportunities to listen to a patient who was bursting to reveal what was on his mind.

The question of training nurses in the direction of authenticity is another matter altogether. It seems to call for a radical alteration in their instructors' conception of what nursing education entails. Much learning about what it means to be a nurse occurs informally when students identify with the attitudes and practices displayed by their teachers. If these teachers are impersonal and have an air of perfection and imperturbability about them, the students are likely to pursue this impossible pinnacle of human performance. If the teacher has a "classroom manner" similar to her bedside manner, then it is difficult to see how the student can ever come to care about her own real self, much less the real self of her patients. One evaluates his real self in the manner that significant others evaluate it. If one's teachers are impersonal in their transactions to students, likely the students will be impersonal in their attitude toward themselves. If their teachers no longer practice active personalized nursing care, but only preach about it, the students likely acquire the concept that teaching is the thing and nursing care is for flunkies. As the teachers are, so will the students become, with the exception of those rebellious students who become their teachers in reverse.

We are beginning to discover that basically normal people can become sensitized and more alert to their own real selves, as well as the real-self expressions of others, without recourse to intensive psychotherapy or technical books on psychodynamics. In fact, the two kinds of alertness seem to grow together. Possibly then, if all nurses who are in an instructional role become less afraid to disclose themselves as persons to their students and proceed to do so, the students will acquire more realistic and feasible role models with which to identify. If teachers will show a greater interest in knowing the real selves of the students whom they teach, they will doubtless foster greater acknowledgement of their real selves by the students. An interest in and an acknowledgment of the full gamut of inner experience in oneself and in others is contagious—just as contagious as is impersonality and indifference to inner experience. It may be proposed as a testable hypothesis that if nursing faculty in colleges and schools become more capable of acknowledging their own inner experience apropos their subject matter and patient contacts, disclosing this to students; and if the faculty acknowledge the feelings of their students, granting them the freedom to have all kinds of feelings; and if the faculty actually practice both nursing and teaching of students on the basis of this greater insight and empathy—then students will learn (or not unlearn) how to be themselves with patients. Doubtless, a regime of this sort would abolish the contrived, tense, even frantic, and sometimes silly specimen of behavior that we have called the bedside manner.

21

Patients Are Persons As Well As Disease-Packages

Educators in the health professions have sought to "integrate" concepts from the disciplines of psychology, sociology, and psychiatry into their basic curricula, presumably with a view toward improving the quality of professional practice. Doubtless, this concern is an outgrowth of discontent on the part of professional person and client alike with the often impersonal nature of professional care. In medicine and nursing, toward which professions this chapter is primarily directed, there is a further reason for concern with "integration." I have reference here to the increasing conviction, based on experience of psychotherapists, that a patient's "self" and the nature of the physician-patient and nurse-patient *relationship* are factors in the patient's illness and recovery.

When we look afresh at the unwieldy jargon of the "integration" assignment (professional educators seem to be no different from other disciplines in their predilection for untranslatable technical terms), we are impelled to inquire, "What is a mental health concept? A psychiatric concept? How does one go about integrating these things? How can anyone tell when integration has been accomplished?" As a matter of fact, I once paralyzed for several minutes the proceedings of a conference in nursing that was devoted to discussion of ways and means of "integrating" merely by raising those questions. Happily enough, the questions were tabled, and the conference got down to its proper business of discussion.

In my work at a nursing college, I addressed myself to the questions inherent in the problem of "integrating mental health concepts," and I have arrived at a direction of thinking which seems to hold some promise of answering these questions in a workable and feasible way. I sought to look at the professional-person-client relationship from a viewpoint sufficiently detached to enable me to identify pertinent variables in just what it was that the educators wanted from "mental health" disciplines—mainly psychiatry and psychology. Furthermore, I tried to ascertain what these disciplines actually had to offer. The present chapter is an attempt to outline a working conception of what mental health disciplines have to offer medicine and nursing, together with some suggestions regarding the manner and manipulation of their "integration."

Let us first look at man. He can readily be "dissected," both conceptually and literally, into a number of component systems, e.g., his circulatory system, endocrine system, nervous system, excretory system, etc. Student of these "systems"—specialists—provide the beginning or the general practitioner with knowledge of the range within which the respective organs and functions vary in wellness and disease. The practitioner is then able, with a given patient, to observe and measure these systems, employing the observations for the diagnosis of illness and as criteria for progress in treatment. The nonspecializing practitioner doesn't know all there is to know about each system, but he doesn't have to; he does, however, know that his job calls for him to be acquainted with some knowledge of these systems, and he conscientiously observes them when he is making routine observations on any patient. Routinely, most physicians will check a patient's pulse and temperature, because it has been learned that the behavior of the heart and the body temperature are sensitive indices of the degree of wellness of the entire body. Such routine attention to these phenomena doubtless illustrates the successful "integration of physiological concepts into medical education and practice."

Psychological science has addressed itself to systematic study of man's inner experience and his overt behavior. These comprise the psychologist's dependent variables, and he investigates their dependence upon myriads of pertinent independent variables. Behavioristic psychologists limit themselves primarily to the analysis of the *stimulus* control of behavior and their findings have something to offer a clinical practitioner. The "phenomenological" psychologists[17]—those concerned with man's subjective side, i.e., with his "self," his inner experience—have convincingly shown that man responds, not to stimuli per se, but rather to the *meanings* which stimuli have for him. These psychologists use the term *phenomenal field** to describe the sum total of a man's conscious experience at any given moment. The phenomenal field includes an individual's perceptions, beliefs, imaginings, and memories, and it also includes a system of cognitions called the *self-structure*.[55] This latter term refers to the beliefs, feelings, and ideals which an individual holds with regard to his own personality. I would like to propose that this complex perceptual-cognitive system—the phenomenal field —is the *variable* which, when "integrated" into medical and nursing curricula and practice, will bring about the outcomes which educators have sought, viz., more personalized care of patients, more apt diagnoses, and more effective therapy. While much of what follows seems obvious, yet I am convinced that the explicit statement of the obvious has value, if for no other reason than to permit critical assessment. Furthermore, the manner in which the

*Also called "phenomenological field," "life space," "situation" etc.

exposition develops throws light on the ways in which "integration" might be accomplished.

We have asserted that man's phenomenal field is a crucial variable in man's behavior. This clearly implies that if we would understand man's overt behavior, *we must become acquainted with the contents of his phenomenal field.* We are obliged to learn what he is thinking and feeling and what the things in the world mean to him. It is also pertinent to assert that *man's phenomenal field affects and is affected by the functioning of the various anatomical and physiological systems.* Circulation, respiration, blood chemistry, and other systems are known to vary with the emotional state of man.

Thus, if a man's behavior and overall physical condition are to be fully understood, we must pay due attention to his phenomenal field. This raises the question, "How does one get to know a person's phenomenal field?" If we regard the phenomenal field as a species of gauge, or recording instrument, we can ask, "How does a practitioner make readings?"

It is possible to guess at a man's probable inner experience—this is what empathy entails—but guessing is rather unreliable. A more direct, perhaps the most direct, means of obtaining "readings" from a man's phenomenal field is to encourage and permit the man to disclose in words and gestures just what he is experiencing, what he sees, feels, believes, and remembers. A person's *self-disclosures* constitute the equivalent of the numbers on a thermometer; the disclosures are the person's attempt to communicate to the doctor or nurse just how the world and his body seem to him. There is reason to suspect that the phenomenal field is an even more sensitive indicator or gauge of the overall condition of a person than, say, the pulse rate. Now, anyone who can count can take a pulse reading. Anyone who can hear can take a phenomenal-field "reading." But all data, whether tracings from an EK, numbers from a manometer, or the self-disclosures of a patient, call for recording and interpretation before they can be employed helpfully in diagnosis and assessment of progress in therapeutic treatment. Consequently, data of all kinds are kept on records.

Anyone who can write can make entries in a medical record; but it takes training and sophistication to be able to "make sense" of the entries that have been made.

With respect to employing phenomenal-field "readings" in medical and nursing practice, two problems arise: (a) how to encourage and permit a patient to disclose his inner experience fully, spontaneously, and truthfully, and (b) how to interpret what has been disclosed. Broadly speaking, a person will disclose himself to an interested auditor who is warm, permissive, and concerned. Skill in eliciting and reinforcing self-disclosure can be learned, and it is already being taught in college courses in interviewing technique. (Witness the increasing widespread use of the "reflection" technique.) Skill in *interpreting the meaning* (manifest and latent) of disclosures, both verbal and nonverbal, can be learned, but it calls for extensive grounding in various basic disciplines, e.g., sociology, psychoanalysis, and personality theory.

But let us look briefly at self-disclosure. Every person has the capacity to disclose the contents of his phenomenal field on request, unless these contents conflict with his self-concept, his public self, or his conscience. Under the latter conditions, disclosure may be highly threatening, and the person may refuse to disclose himself openly, honestly, and spontaneously. In most general terms, we may say that anxiety makes a person reluctant to disclose the contents of his phenomenal field to someone else. This implies that a professional person, such as a nurse, teacher, physician, or psychotherapist, must learn ways of recognizing and coping with the anxieties that inhibit self-disclosure. However, in our culture, people withhold self-disclosure for another, more obvious reason; they believe (often erroneously) that no one is interested in their unique view of the world, their thoughts and feelings. Consequently they keep this information to themselves, disclosing only banalities and clichés. If a nurse or teacher conveys a sincere interest in learning what is on the mind of the patient or student, then this reason for avoiding fuller disclosure can easily be bypassed.

It is the thesis of this chapter that "mental health and psychiatric concepts" will have been integrated into health professions' curricula and practice when "readings" from the psychological "gauge"—self-disclosures from the patient—are as routinely obtained, recorded, evaluated, and acted upon as are readings of temperature or blood pressure, or observations of the patients' bandages. *When the phenomenal field is not "checked" routinely in nursing or medicine, a crime of omission is committed, the gravity of which is no less serious than failure to make routine physiological checks.* A patient's phenomenal field constitutes information that may be highly crucial in arriving at a diagnosis or in planning therapy. This information is not only pertinent at the time when a "history" is being taken; the phenomenal field goes on registering thoughts, feelings, fantasies, memories, and perceptions, even when a patient is asleep. In this regard, it is little different from the heart, which continues to beat twenty-four hours daily and which is routinely checked every time a physician encounters a patient. When a professional person of any sort is face to face with his client, he is maximally helpful when he refreshes his concept of the client's condition. This means making all observations that will be pertinent. There is little basis for assuming that the patient is exactly the same from hour to hour, and so fresh observations are called for with every contact. This means that self-disclosure should be obtained—the phenomenal field should be checked—every time that a professional person is face to face with his client. The information obtained from a patient's disclosures can then be evaluated in its own right or correlated with other data that are available, e.g., physiological measures of one kind or another. Thus, in response to the question "How do you feel?," a patient may say, "I feel just fine," but one may then find his pulse racing, his blood pressure high, etc. Discrepancies of this sort (not unlike a primitive lie detctor) will mean something to the physician or nurse responsible for the patient's well-being.

We have mentioned several times that obtaining self-disclosure from a patient is directly analogous to obtaining data about a patient's blood pressure; the phenomenal field and the sphygmomanometer are both "gauges" which register data of importance to the practitioner. But there is one crucial difference between the processes of obtaining a blood-pressure reading and a phenomenal-self "reading" that must be noted.

Few patients report an increase in well-being following a blood-pressure reading. Many patients, however, will experience a reduction in anxiety and physical tension and an increase in feeling of their own identity and worth following the experience of full self-disclosure to an interested nurse or physician. They feel *understood* at such times[128] As Freud early noted, the technique of observation and the mechanism of helping are well-nigh identical in psychotherapy in particular and in interpersonal transactions in general.

What does one do with "readings from the psychological gauge" —a patient's self-disclosure? For that matter, what does a nurse or physician do with blood-pressure and pulse readings? The latter data are recorded on special charts, they are plotted, and, more imported, they are used as the basis for evaluating the overall condition of the patient and his progress in therapy and as guides to further therapeutic measures. Self-disclosure data has not been as systematically sought, recorded, charted, and evaluated from day to day as have temperature or blood pressure, nor has it been as systematically employed as a means of assessing progress in therapy or as a guide to therapeutic measures—except perhaps accidentally. It should be sought and used!

Suppose I were a physician, glancing over a chart that was kept on a patient. Under the heading "Temperature," I would note the daily fluctuations. Under the heading "Bowel Movements," I might notice that these had been carefully charted and evaluated. Under the heading "Patient's Self" I might notice *nothing*. This would mean something to me. Or I might notice six brief entries made today for Mr. Jones, who is awaiting an operation for cancer of the rectum:

6:30 a.m. Mr. Jones said that he feels fine (during breakfast).
9:00 a.m. As he was receiving an injection, he said, "I feel fine."

12:00 noon Patient reports that he feels just fine.
7:00 p.m. He says that he feels fine.
9:00 p.m. He says that he feels fine.

I might look at what has been entered and wonder why he says he feels fine. I don't know what conclusion I might come to, but noting this data would impel me to make further observations.

It could be that the entries (or lack of entries) for "Patient's Self" might reflect nothing more than the fact that no one has systematically shown an interest in making these "readings"; or the trivial nature of the entries may show (to a skilled person) the presence of profound anxiety that has not been medically acknowledged and coped with. Or lack of entries may betoken grave neglect of important observations on the part of attending personnel.

This leads me to an observation about relationships between professional people. Just as a patient may fear to disclose himself to nurse or physician, so might the nurse dread disclosing or reporting—in person or on paper—what she has observed, felt, guessed, and thought in connection with the patient. She may fear being criticized or laughed at. If such is the case, it could well happen that much possibly invaluable information is lost to the physician because he has not heard or read about these observations and hunches. Just as a patient must disclose his "real self" to his doctors and nurses so that they can be maximally helpful in diagnosis and treatment, *so must all who attend the patient disclose to responsible parties the pertinent aspects of their experience with the patient.* Just as a patient's phenomenal field is a most important instrument for recording and reporting what goes on in his whole life situation, *so is the phenomenal field of the nurse a recording and reporting instrument—often a most sensitive one.* If it is not heard or read by a head nurse or physician, then it is analogous with failure to examine X-rays that have already been made— a loss of possibly important data. Thus, *any factor which inhibits disclosure of self on the part of one professional person to another is detrimental to the overall program of diagnosis and therapy for the patient.*

Let it be taken as proven that observations of a patient's phenomenal field, secured by focused interview or through the promotion of self-disclosure while other aspects of care are carried on, is a necessary condition for optimum care and evidence of the extent of integration of mental-health and psychiatric concepts into general nursing and medical care. It is pertinent to ask, now, "What factors militate against obtaining self-disclosure from patients?"

Perhaps the most general answers to this question are (a) failure of professional people to recognize the importance of phenomenal-field data in an overall program of diagnosis and treatment, and (b) a dread of "becoming too involved" with patients when the latter are permitted to disclose themselves to a full extent. This dread of becoming overly involved has two justifications that doctors and nurses often mention. One is that "There is too much work to be done, and so time cannot be wasted just talking or listening to patients." The other, possibly deeper, reason for blocking self-disclosure in patients is fear of the feelings which patients' disclosures can evoke in the professional person. I would like to comment briefly on the phobia against involvement with patients.

Doctors and nurses often acquire, at some time during their training, the view that to "be professional" means to be without feeling in the face of human misery. Granted, it is of the utmost importance that a physician or nurse not explode into helpless tears or impotent rage when operations are to be performed or difficult diagnoses obtained. But this is not to say that they must be impersonal machines without affect and without the capacity to be affected by the needs and feelings of patients. In the last chapter I noted that the "bedside manner," with its false jollity, or assumed omniscience, omnipotence, and imperturbability, are special cases of "character armor"[95] or a "magic cloak,"[85] donned by nurses and physicians to squelch their own feelings and to squelch self-disclosure in patients.

With respect to failure to recognize the importance of phenomenal-field data for ongoing diagnosis and therapy, it may be said that professional schools may produce such failure by important omissions in their curricula. If the curricular job had been well done, practicing nurses or physicians would *feel guilty* if they did not notice and record pertinent aspects of patients' disclosures, just as they might now feel guilty of oversight if they failed to record pulse, blood pressure, laboratory reports, etc.

The foregoing considerations provide us with a convenient and valid basis for assessing the extent to which any health-profession education program has effectively integrated mental-health and psychiatric concepts into its curriculum. One can look for the following sorts of evidence:

1. To what extent does the professional person strive to learn each patient's "self" or his phenomenal field?
2. How effective is the given professional person in promoting full and pertinent disclosure of self in patients?
3. How sophisticated is the professional person in interpreting or evaluating a patient's disclosure (or lack thereof) as bases for helpful actions or as occasions for seeking consultative help with a patient?
4. What allowance is made for disclosure data in patient charts kept at present for other kinds of information? What is the nature of the entries which are made concerning patient disclosures, if any?
5. How alert is the professional person to evidence of anxiety in a patient which is not so obvious from the verbatim transcript of his conversation?
6. How capable are doctors, nurses, and other health-profession personnel at behaving at a "real-self" level with each other and with patients, avoiding the grotesque phoniness of the bedside manner?
7. How competent are personnel in establishing and maintaining personal contact with patients who come from a diversity of age ranges and cultural backgrounds, who suffer a variety of physical ills, and who represent diverse personality structures?

Direct acknowledgement of the importance of patients' phenomenal fields as a factor in their illness and recovery forcefully directs the attention of educators to aspects of their curriculum which enhance or inhibit students' ability to obtain and cope helpfully with self-disclosure in patients. "Interpersonal skill" or "interpersonal competence" then acquires more explicit meaning; in this context, it implies ability to facilitate disclosure in patients, to acknowledge and interpret what has been disclosed, and to use the information as the basis for more accurately "aimed" professional action. Such action may run the gamut from brief psychotherapy, to a factual lecture, to frank admission of inability to cope with the facts that have been learned. On the latter occasions, the professional person may then call for help from suitable specialists.

Acknowledgement of the importance of patients' phenomenal fields does not necessarily imply that all nurses, physicians, or aides must be fully trained psychotherapists. Psychotherapy is a specialty which seeks to change personality in basic ways, and it calls for special training. However, every practitioner can be trained to recognize the importance of observing patients' inner experience, and every practitioner can be helped to improve in skill at eliciting the necessary self-disclosure. It will be enough for the improvement of overall medical care if all personnel—nurses, physicians, aides, etc.—routinely seek and routinely record disclosures of patients. Such a practice will have a double benefit. Not only will it ensure that crucial information is noted and reported; it will also do much to vitiate the well-founded complaint of many patients that they are impersonally treated by health-profession personnel. Thus, it will strike positively at one source of the latent hostility which the lay public holds for medicine and nursing.

22

To Whom Can a Nurse
Give Personalized Care?

It has become customary in most professions to classify practitioners into various specialties, and the nonspecialist is regarded as a
"general practitioner" of his profession. In nursing, one speaks of
nursing educators, nursing supervisors, psychiatric nurses, obstetri-
cal nurses, medical-surgical nurses, and the like. These are convenient labels describing the place where the given nurse works and
the broad categories into which her clients—patients, students, or
other nurses—may be assigned. In spite of their convenience, I
believe that these classification labels encourage a kind of unhelp-
ful confusion in thinking, teaching, and practice. We tend to
think that there is something special and basically different about
psychiatric nursing, or OB nursing, or pediatric nursing, and I

would like to propose that any differences are superficial, and they mask something basic that is common to all branches of nursing.

The "something basic" which is common to all phases of nursing, and for that matter to all helping professions, is the dedication of oneself to helping the other fellow achieve worthwhile objectives—health, comfort, freedom from pain and suffering, the dissipation of ignorance, etc. Anyone who wants to be a helper needs good will and a certain basic skill. This skill has been called "interpersonal competence."[27] Interpersonal competence means the ability to produce desirable and valued outcomes to one's transactions with people.

In the practice of caring for patients, interpersonal competence is, of course, necessary. Nurses who have achieved this kind of competence are able to achieve desirable outcomes to their transactions with patients, and *their patients therefore must show signs of the quality of care that has been given.* What does a well-nursed patient look like, and how does he differ from one who has not been well nursed? I am afraid that in the welter of studies published in professional nursing journals, not many have focused on the patient as the yardstick or gauge of nursing competence. Perhaps that will be the next stage of nursing research—to devise measures of patients' behavior, inner experience, and physical status that will correlate with measures of nurses' behavior, training and personality.

Let us pretend that we have already solved the problem of defining, describing, and measuring a well-nursed patient. We can assume he is as comfortable as his condition permits, he knows why he became ill and what is being done for him, he feels his nurses really care what happens to him, he knows *that they know him as a unique person* because they took the trouble to learn about him, and he knows he told them much about himself. He feels free to call for help when he wants it, and does so. His nurse "tunes in" on him at regular intervals to sample his private, personal, psychological world as it were—not with an empty question, "How do we feel"—and she uses this information as the basis of actions which make him say "ah-h-h!" He wants to get well and to get back into the community, and if his place in the community is one which imposes a lot of sickness-producing stress on him, the nurse has found this out and conveyed the information to a social worker, or the physician, or somebody who might be able to help improve the situation.

Who is this nurse who has been able to display such competence? And what are the characteristics of the patient which permitted the nurse to produce just those wonderful outcomes? At this point, I want to introduce a different concept of specialists and general practitioners in nursing. A specialist in nursing, according to this different view, is someone who can feel an identity with and become concerned about the needs and wants of only a very small class of patients. An extreme case of a nursing specialist would be a nurse who could establish contact with and provide personalized care only for girls aged twenty from her neighborhood in Palatka. Everyone else is a threat, a mystery, an object of distrust, disgust, or indifference to her. These other people—and they include everyone else in the world but twenty-year-old girls from her neighborhood in Palatka—are treated as objects, as categories, as things, but not as people. The extreme specialist of this sort may have the identical number of nonpersonal nursing skills as a general nursing expert has, but she can apply them in the context of a person-to-person contact, producing optimum outcomes only with this very narrow range of patients. Patients outside the restricted range are a puzzle or a threat to her, and she doesn't want to get to know them. She takes care of their bodies, but not their whole selves.

Let us play awhile with this idea of nursing specialists. Remember, we are talking here about nurses who have received standard minimum training, so that they can do all the technical things that nurses are expected to be able to do. But we are also talking about the ability to produce in a patient the feeling of being understood, because he is understood; the feeling that his nurse cares for and about him, because she does; the feeling of comfort that follows care above the call of duty, whatever that means. Any nurse can stick a needle or an enema into anything human and, for that matter, into beings which are not human. But not all nurses can supply optimum care as we have outlined it to all patients.

Now, to illustrate. There are nurses who cannot care for patients who are known to be immoral. One of our students mentioned that, in taking care of some young mothers of illegitimate children who were having their babies in a local hospital, she would stay a minimum length of time and get out of the room as fast as she could. We can call this girl a goodness specialist.

There are white nurses who cannot care for Negro patients. Let us call these nurses "white specialists."

There are nurses who are repelled by sex and who balk at taking care of patients who make passes. We might call these specialists "nurses of neuters."

There are nurses who cannot take care of people whose behavior is at first bizarre and incomprehensible, as is sometimes true of so-called psychiatric patients. We might call these nurses "normality specialists."

There are nurses who can do what is called for only with patients unconscious on the operating table. A conscious patient induces anxiety, threat, bashfulness, etc. We might call these nurses "coma specialists."

There are nurses who can care only for Protestants. Catholics, Jews, Hindus, agnostics, and Zen Buddhists arouse their anxiety and indignation, and they provide only minimum care for people in these categories. We might call these nurses "Protestant specialists."

I think that by now you have grasped the meaning I intend with this different concept of specialist. Simply stated, these specialists are nurses who can provide personalized, warm, responsive care, prompted by spontaneous concern, for only a small segment of humanity. Everyone outside the segment only gets impersonal care—strangers doing things to strangers.

What, then, is a general nursing practitioner? This is an ideal that is never achieved by any particular nurse, but it is useful as a goal toward which to aim. A general nursing practitioner is a person who is able to get into empathic contact with anybody who is sick, whether white or Negro, young or old, Protestant or Catholic, moral or immoral. If she cannot immediately understand this very patient, she strives to learn his language, his view of the world, his values, his wants, so that she can then care for him. She cares about *people*, not just one narrow segment of the population, and she wants to know them, help them, and be an effective agent in their recovery toward comfort and wellness.

Who is this paragon? A better question is, who has the greatest chances of becoming such a growing paragon who broadens her range of competence with each person nursed? The becoming general nursing practitioner is a person who is open to her own experience, who genuinely cares about people and about herself. This is important. She cares about herself. The proof of effective caring about oneself is a self which is happy, growing, open. A person who cares about himself has been cared for in the past and is being cared about in the present by others. This person is free then to care about others.

This paragon is a person who is always in process of maturing and growing. What I mean by this is she can look into her own memory and experience and find that she has suffered, thought, felt, wished, and enjoyed just about everything human beings anywhere under the sun have experienced. This openness to herself makes it possible for her to establish empathic contact with the patients as they come and go. She realizes that each patient is unique, and that *there is no automatic, easy way to take care of individual patients*—only of people who fall into a category and who have thus lost all vestiges of individuality. Consequently, she never assumes that she knows a patient before she has taken steps to become acquainted and reacquainted with the reality of his self, his inner experience.

Every one is a specialist of one sort or another, but this is a fact of life, not a condemnation. Nobody but God is a full-fledged general practitioner of nursing—that is, able to love everyone in the active sense (though some people seem to think that God loves only the people in their club).

The more that you experience as a person inside a sickroom and in outside life, the more progress you make toward general practice. The more suffering, enjoying, sinning, being afraid, becoming psychotic and recovering, being sick, reading books, having babies, fighting and arguing, loving and making up, daydreaming you do—in short, living and learning about yourself—the more you move toward general practice.

Now what I just said can be stated another way. The more you grow as a person, the less shocked you become about people who are different from yourself. And in many ways, the more you grow, the more different and the more similar you become to everyone. I say similar because with living come the feelings, hopes, fears, doubts, joys, and sorrows that all humans share because they are human. I say different because every single person is a variation on the human theme and commands respect for his difference.

Actually, there is something about training that can actively obstruct growth toward general practice. This is the view that practice makes perfect and that repeated practice makes for effortlessness. We live in what I call the "Fat Society"; we worship the idol called ease. Now there is point in becoming efficient and even unconscious in the performance of standard skills, like injections, bed-making, and so on, because the speed and effectiveness frees time for other pursuits. But let me push the cult of effortless nursing to its logical extreme. Let us pretend that, through scientific busywork, we could construct an automatized hospital. I will outline what it would be like.

Each patient lies in his own cubicle with wires attached to his head, his muscles, his viscera. The wires are electronic pickups which transmit signals to a computer whenever a patient's bladder is full, his bowel stuffed, or he is hungry or in pain. Then, the computer "orders" different kinds of apparatus to empty the bladder and bowel, fill the stomach, scratch the itch, massage the back, and so on. We could even mount each bed on a slowly moving belt; the patient gets in a bed at one end, four or six days later his bed reaches the exit, and the patient is healed—we hope. Certainly a dream (or nightmare) factory of this sort would solve the technical problems and the legwork problems which many nurses either complain about or delegate to auxiliary personnel. But what would the nurses do with their time then? And what would the patients be like?

About the only thing that such machines cannot provide is human warmth, love, and responsive care. Do patients need this? Or do they merely need sanitary surroundings, medicine, and rest?

Patients get sick because their bodies, at one time fairly sterile environments for cells, bacteria, and viruses, suddenly become very fertile, as if fertilized, and the alien cells and germs grow like weeds. When does this happen? Recent research findings suggest that illness begins when a person's life begins to lose zest, a sense of future, meaning, and love.[23, 41, 110, 131] When one's relationships with people become impersonal, a stage of vague depression or a drop in spirits takes place, the person loses hope, and sickness will begin unless there is a change in the way the person sees the situation. People become well not alone because of the medicines they take, but because of the meaning the medicines have for the patient. The patient has faith in medicine, doctors, and all the symbols and rituals of the modern hospital. If the patient has faith neither in doctors nor in hospitals, he will likely fail and die.

One of the events which we believe inspires faith and hope in a patient is the conviction that somebody cares about him. If this proves true, it implies that the quality of the nurse-patient relationship is a factor in the patient's recovery. Direct contact with a patient somehow increases his sense of being a worthwhile individual person, and this experience inspirits him—it does something to the body which helps it throw off illness.

Sincere attempts to know and to understand a patient and to help him be comfortable increase his sense of identity and integrity, and this experience seems to be a factor in healing.

On the other hand, contempt, indifference, insincerity, and impersonal relationships with patients undermine their sense of self and identity and make them feel like nobodies. Perhaps some nurses are experts at making all patients feel like nobodies by "treating them all alike," like robots or piles of meat.

It seems to me that "personal nursing" is something that machines cannot do; but it also seems to me that nurses, in their efforts to make their practice of care efficient, impersonal, and effortless, are actually competing with machines, and becoming machinelike in the process. Even the most impersonal of nurses, however, becomes human when she is called on to treat some patient who falls within the range of her specialty—the splinter of humanity which she regards as human. Hopefully, nursing practitioners will soon learn that nursing is a special case of loving.

A TECHNICAL APPENDIX
FOR PSYCHOLOGISTS

A Research Approach
to Self-Disclosure*

BY SIDNEY M. JOURARD AND PAUL LASAKOW†

The present paper describes a questionnaire method for measuring
the amount and content of self-disclosure to selected "target-
persons," and reports the results of three exploratory studies. Self-
disclosure refers to the process of making the self known to other
persons; "target-persons" are persons to whom information about
the self is communicated.

The process of self-disclosure has been studied by others from
various points of view. Block[7] and Block and Bennett[8] have demon-

*Reprinted from the *Journal of Abnormal and Social Psychology*, Vol. 56,
No. 1, January, 1958.
†The authors are indebted to Drs. A. J. Riopelle, Emory University, and O.
Lacy, University of Alabama, for statistical advice.

strated that the content of communication about the self is a function of variations in "own-role." Lewin[75] noted differences between typical Germans and Americans regarding their readiness to confide personal information to others. Jourard[55] has suggested that accurate portrayal of the self to others is an identifying criterion of healthy personality, while neurosis is related to inability to know one's "real self" and to make it known to others. Characterological studies of Fromm,[33] Riesman,[99] and Horney[44] have called attention to a tendency common among persons in our society, to misrepresent the self to others. This tendency is central to the "marketing personality," the "other-directed character," and the "self-alienated" individual, as these have been described by their respective authors. Since much of social science is founded upon the self-disclosures of respondents, the conditions and dimensions of self-disclosure bear directly upon the validity of many purported facts in the social sciences.

From the foregoing, it may be concluded that systematic analysis of self-disclosure holds promise of yielding information that is relevant to diverse areas of theory and method.

The following questions were proposed for investigation:

1. Do subjects (Ss) vary in the extent to which they disclose themselves to different target persons, for example, mother, father, male friend, and female friend? What is the effect of the Ss' marital status on self-disclosure to parents and friends? What is the effect of the Ss' feelings and attitudes toward particular target-persons upon self-disclosure to them? The last question was investigated only with respect to the relationship between Ss' disclosure of self to parents, and their feelings and attitudes toward their parents.

2. Are there differences between categories of information about the self (aspects of self) with respect to self-disclosure? Do Ss tend to disclose some aspects of self more fully than others?

3. Are there differences ascertainable between Negro and white Ss with respect to self-disclosure?

4. Are there sex differences regarding self-disclosure?

INSTRUMENTS

The Self-Disclosure Questionnaire

A sixty-item questionnaire was devised. As can be seen in Table 1, the items are classified in groups of ten within each of six more general categories of information about the self (aspects). Ss were given the following instruction for completing the questionnaire:

The answer-sheet which you have been given has columns with the headings "Mother," "Father," "Male Friend," "Female Friend," and "Spouse." You are to read each item on the questionnaire, and then indicate on the answer-sheet the extent that you have talked about that item to each person; that is, the extent to which you have made yourself known to that person. Use the rating-scale that you see on the answer sheet to describe the extent that you have talked about each item.

TABLE 1

THE SELF-DISCLOSURE QUESTIONNAIRE

Attitudes and Opinions

1. What I think and feel about religion; my personal religious views.
2. My personal opinions and feelings about other religious groups than my own, e.g., Protestants, Catholics, Jews, atheists.
3. My views on communism.
4. My views on the present government—the president, government, policies, etc.
5. My views on the question of racial integration in schools, transportation, etc.
6. My personal views on drinking.
7. My personal views on sexual morality—how I feel that I and others ought to behave in sexual matters.
8. My personal standards of beauty and attractiveness in women— what I consider to be attractive in a woman.

9. The things that I regard as desirable for a man to be—what I look for in a man.
10. My feeling about how parents ought to deal with children.

Tastes and Interests

1. My favorite foods, the ways I like food prepared, and my food dislikes.
2. My favorite beverages, and the ones I don't like.
3. My likes and dislikes in music.
4. My favorite reading matter.
5. The kinds of movies that I like to see best; the TV shows that are my favorites.
6. My tastes in clothing.
7. The style of house, and the kinds of furnishings that I like best.
8. The kind of party, or social gathering that I like best, and the kind that would bore me, or that I wouldn't enjoy.
9. My favorite ways of spending spare time, e.g., hunting, reading, cards, sports events, parties, dancing, etc.
10. What I would appreciate most for a present.

Work (or studies)

1. What I find to be the worst pressures and strains in my work.
2. What I find to be the most boring and unenjoyable aspects of my work.
3. What I enjoy most, and get the most satisfaction from in my present work.

TABLE 1 (Continued)

Work (or studies) (Continued)

4. What I feel are my shortcomings and handicaps that prevent me from working as I'd like to, or that prevent me from getting further ahead in my work.
5. What I feel are my special strong points and qualifications for my work.
6. How I feel that my work is appreciated by others (e.g., boss, fellow-workers, teacher, husband, etc.)
7. My ambitions and goals in my work.
8. My feelings about the salary or rewards that I get for my work.
9. How I feel about the choice of career that I have made—whether or not I'm satisfied with it.
10. How I really feel about the people that I work for, or work with.

Money

1. How much money I make at my work, or get as an allowance.
2. Whether or not I owe money; if so, *how much*.
3. Whom I owe money to at present; or whom I have borrowed from in the past.
4. Whether or not I have savings, and the amount.
5. Whether or not others owe me money; the amount, and who owes it to me.
6. Whether or not I gamble; if so, the way I gamble, and the extent of it.
7. All of my present sources of income—wages, fees, allowance, dividends, etc.
8. My total financial worth, including property, savings, bonds, insurance, etc.
9. My most pressing need for money right now, e.g., outstanding bills, some major purchase that is desired or needed.
10. How I budget my money—the proportion that goes to necessities, luxuries, etc.

Personality

1. The aspects of my personality that I dislike, worry about, that I regard as a handicap to me.
2. What feelings, if any, that I have trouble expressing or controlling.
3. The facts of my present sex life—including knowledge of how I get sexual gratification; any problems that I might have; with whom I have relations, if anybody.
4. Whether or not I feel that I am attractive to the opposite sex; my problems, if any, about getting favorable attention from the opposite sex.

Personality (Continued)

5. Things in the past or present that I feel ashamed and guilty about.
6. The kinds of things that make me just furious.
7. What it takes to get me feeling real depressed or blue.
8. What it takes to get me real worried, anxious, and afraid.
9. What it takes to hurt my feelings deeply.
10. The kinds of things that make me especially proud of myself, elated, full of self-esteem or self-respect.

Body

1. My feelings about the appearance of my face—things I don't like, and things that I might like about my face and head—nose, eyes, hair, teeth, etc.
2. How I wish I looked: my ideals for overall appearance.
3. My feelings about different parts of my body—legs, hips, waist, weight, chest or bust, etc.
4. Any problems and worries that I had with my appearance in the past.
5. Whether or not I now have any health problems—e.g., trouble with sleep, digestion, female complaints, heart condition, allergies, headaches, piles, etc.
6. Whether or not I have any long-range worries or concerns about my health, e.g., cancer, ulcers, heart trouble.
7. My past record of illness and treatment.
8. Whether or not I now make special effort to keep fit, healthy, and attractive, e.g., calisthenics, diet.
9. My present physical measurements, e.g., height, weight, waist, etc.
10. My feelings about my adequacy in sexual behavior—whether or not I feel able to perform adequately in sex-relationships.

The self-disclosure rating-scale was as follows:

0: Have told the other person nothing about this aspect of me.

1: Have talked in general terms about this item. The other person has only a general idea about this aspect of me.

2: Have talked in full and complete detail about this item to the other person. He knows me fully in this respect, and could describe me accurately.

X: Have lied or misrepresented myself to the other person so that he has a false picture of me.

The numerical entries were summed (X's were counted as zeros), yielding totals which constituted the self-disclosure scores.

Seventy white unmarried college students of both sexes were tested for self-disclosure to Mother, Father, Male Friend, and Female Friend, in a study of reliability. Since the questionnaire included 60 items, and there were four target-persons, a total of 240 entries were made by each S. These 240 entries were divided into halves by the odd-even method, and the subtotal sums were correlated with each other. The resultant r, corrected, was .94, indicating that the Ss were responding consistently to the questionnaire over all target persons, and all aspects of self.

Parent-Cathexis questionnaires. Mother-cathexis and Father-cathexis questionnaires, fully described elsewhere,[53] were employed to test Ss' feelings toward their parents. The Ss rated their feelings about 40 parental traits, e.g., *sense of humor, temper, ability to make decisions*, in accordance with the following scale:

1: Have strong positive feelings; like very much.
2: Have moderate positive feelings.
3: Have no feelings one way or the other.
4: Have moderate negative feelings.
5: Have strong negative feelings; dislike very much.

High scores indicated negative feelings toward the parents, while low scores signified positive feelings.

SUBJECTS

The Ss included in the studies to be reported were taken from larger samples drawn from three Alabama college populations: two white liberal arts colleges, a Negro liberal arts college, and a school of nursing located at a medical school. For the combined sample 300 white and Negro liberal arts college sophomores and juniors were obtained, and 55 white nursing students. All Ss were tested in groups by an examiner of the same race.

For the purpose of analysis, the following randomly selected subsamples were drawn from the combined samples:

1. From the 300 liberal arts students, a subsample of 10 white males, 10 white females, 10 Negro males, and 10 Negro females was drawn for the study of differences in self-disclosure associated with race, sex, targets, and aspects of self. All Ss were unmarried, and, in all cases, the parents were living. Mean ages were: white males, 21.70, SD 2.00; white females, 20.30, SD .90; Negro males, 22.10, SD 2.02; and Negro females, 20.40, SD .45. All Ss had

been tested for self-disclosure to Mother, Father, Male Friend, and Female Friend.

2. From all the white respondents in the combined sample, a subsample of 10 married male and 10 married female Ss was drawn for comparison with the first subsample of 10 unmarried males and 10 unmarried females to test the effects of marriage on self-disclosure patterns. These Ss had indicated self-disclosure to Mother, Father, Same-sex Friend, and Spouse. Mean age for the married males was 23.40, SD 1.43, and for the married females, 20.60, SD 2.42.

3. Thirty-one unmarried nursing students comprised the third sample, used to examine the relationship between parent-cathexis and self-disclosure to the parents. Mean age for this group was 18.59, SD 3.53.

The data were analyzed according to Lindquist's[76] Type VI model for analysis of variance with mixed "between-within" effects. Critical differences for t ratios at the .01 level were computed between all groups, targets, and aspects of self when F ratios proved significant. Pearsonian r's were computed between Mother-cathexis scores and scores for disclosure to the mother, and between Father-cathexis scores and the corresponding disclosure scores, within the group of 31 nursing students to whom these two instrument had been administered.

RESULTS

Influence of Race, Sex, Target-Differences, and Aspects of Self

Table 2 shows the results of analysis of variance of the self-disclosure scores of the 40 white and Negro Ss, while Fig. 1 portrays mean self-disclosure scores classified by targets, groups, and aspects of self. The findings may be summarized as follows:

1. The four groups differed in total self-disclosure. Table 3 shows that the white Ss disclosed more than the Negroes, and the females more than the males.

TABLE 2

ANALYSIS OF VARIANCE OF SELF-DISCLOSURE SCORES OF WHITE
AND NEGRO, MALE AND FEMALE SUBJECTS

Source	Mean Square	df	Error Term	F
Between Groups	892.33	3	Error(b)	6.78†
Males vs. Females	573.50	1		4.36*
White vs. Negros	2076.82	1		15.78†
Sex × Race	126.67	1		
Error(b)	131.61	36		
Total df Between		39		
(Within-Groups Comparisons)				
Between Target-Persons	557.06	3	$Error_1(w)$	10.89†
Between Aspects of Self	952.01	5	$Error_2(w)$	40.39†
Target × Aspect	87.49	15	$Error_3(w)$	15.38†
Group × Target	128.11	9	$Error_1(w)$	2.50*
Group × Aspect	32.16	15	$Error_2(w)$	1.36
Group × Target × Aspect	9.61	45	$Error_3(w)$	1.69*
Total df Within		92		
$Error_1(w)$	51.17	108		
$Error_2(w)$	23.57	180		
$Error_3(w)$	5.69	540		
Total Error df		828		
Total df		959		

* $p < .05$.
† $p < .001$.

2. The combined group of 40 Ss varied in amount of self-disclosure to different persons. They disclosed the most to Mother, and in lesser amount to Father, Male Friend, and Female Friend, as shown in Table 4. Sex- and race-differences in disclosure to the four target-persons is shown clearly in Fig. 1. Noteworthy is the consistently lower amounts of self-disclosure to Father on the part of Negro Ss.

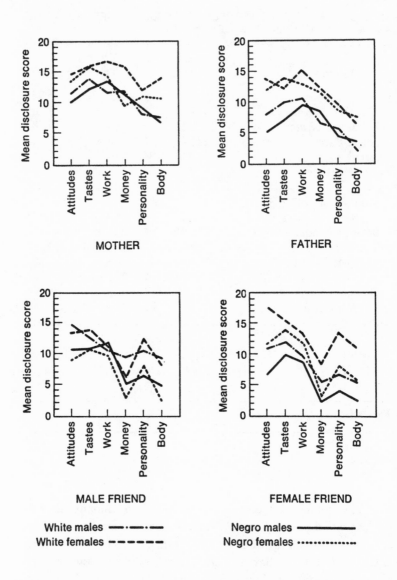

Figure 1 Mean Self-Disclosure of White and Negro, Male and Female Ss to Mother, Father, Male Friend, and Female Friend.

TABLE 3

DIFFERENCES BETWEEN GROUPS IN MEAN DISCLOSURE SCORES

			Differences†		
Group	Mean*	SD	Negro Males	White Females	Negro Females
White Males	248.50	68.60	+62.60	−45.10	+33.50
Negro Males	185.90	36.10		−107.70	−19.10
White Females	293.60	45.20			+78.60
Negro Females	215.00	57.60			

* Highest possible score, 480.
† Critical difference for $t = 2.72$, $p < .01$, $df = 36$ is 13.95 (cf. 76, p. 93).
All differences are thus significant at $p < .01$.

3. The combined group of 40 Ss varied in self-disclosure according to aspects of self. Table 5 shows that two cluster of aspects appeared—a "high disclosure" cluster comprised of Tastes and Interests, Attitudes and Opinions, and Work, and a "low disclosure" cluster that included Money, Personality, and Body.

4. There was significant interaction between targets and aspects, groups and targets, and groups, targets, and aspects. The group-by-aspect interaction was not significant.

TABLE 4

DIFFERENCES BETWEEN TARGETS IN MEAN DISCLOSURE SCORES

			Differences†		
Group	Mean*	SD	Father	Male Friend	Female Friend
Mother	72.30	19.50	+20.60‡	+17.21‡	+16.72‡
Father	51.70	24.13		−3.48	−4.88‡
Male Friend	55.18	22.43			1.40
Female Friend	56.58	27.70			

* Highest possible score, 120.
† Critical difference for $t = 2.63$, $p < .01$, $df = $ ‹08 is 4.21 (cf. 76, p. 93).
‡ $p < .01$.

TABLE 5

DIFFERENCES BETWEEN TARGETS IN MEAN DISCLOSURE SCORES
ASPECTS OF SELF‡

Aspect	Mean	SD	Tastes	Work	Money	Pers.	Body
					Differences†		
Att.	45.35	14.20	−4.93‡	−2.30	+13.12‡	+11.30‡	+19.15‡
Tastes	50.28	13.98		+2.63	+18.05‡	+16.23‡	+24.08‡
Work	47.65	13.65			+15.42‡	+13.60‡	+21.45‡
Money	32.23	15.65				−1.82	+6.03‡
Pers.	34.05	13.45					+7.85
Body‡	26.20	14.28					

* Highest possible score, 80.
† Critical Difference for $t = 2.63$, $p < .01$, $df = 180$, is 2.87 (cf. 76, p. 93).
‡ $p < .01$.

TABLE 6

ANALYSIS OF VARIANCE OF SELF-DISCLOSURE SCORES OF
MARRIED AND UNMARRIED MALES

Source	Mean Square	df	Error Term	F
Between Groups	37.95	1	Error(b)	.17
Error(b)	228.81	18		
Total df Between		19		
(Within-Groups Comparisons)				
Between Target-Persons	232.99	3	Error$_1$(w)	6.10*
Between Aspects of Self	477.49	5	Error$_2$(w)	24.80†
Target × Aspect	21.72	15	Error$_3$(w)	4.19†
Group × Target	676.95	3	Error$_1$(w)	17.72†
Group × Aspect	1.00	5	Error$_2$(w)	.00
Group × Target × Aspect	22.24	15	Error$_3$(w)	4.49†
Total df Within		46		
Error$_1$(w)	38.21	54		
Error$_2$(w)	19.25	90		
Error$_3$(w)	4.95	270		
Total Error df		414		
Total df		479		

* $p < .01$.
† $p < .001$.

TABLE 7

ANALYSIS OF VARIANCE OF SELF-DISCLOSURE SCORES OF
MARRIED AND UNMARRIED FEMALES

Source	Mean Square	df	Error Term	F
Between Groups	186.25	1	Error(b)	1.38
Error(b)	135.27	18		
Total df Between		19		
(Within-Groups Comparisons)				
Between Target-Persons	349.90	3	$Error_1(w)$	6.08*
Between Aspects of Self	345.54	5	$Error_2(w)$	18.91†
Target × Aspect	46.64	15	$Error_3(w)$	8.00†
Group × Target	531.48	3	$Error_1(w)$	9.23†
Group × Aspect	15.63	5	$Error_2(w)$	.86
Group × Target × Aspect	26.01	15	$Error_3(w)$	4.46†
Total df Within		46		
$Error_1(w)$	57.56	54		
$Error_2(w)$	18.27	90		
$Error_3(w)$	5.83	270		
Total Error df		414		
Total df		479		

* $p < .01$.
† $p < .001$.

Influence of Marriage

Separate analyses of variance compared married with unmarried
males, and married with unmarried females. The results are shown
in Table 6, for males, and Table 7, for females. In the analyses,
Opposite-sex Friend and Spouse were treated as equivalent target-
persons.

No differences were found between married and unmarried Ss
in total amount of self-disclosure. Figs. 2 and 3 show, however,
that: (a) married Ss disclosed less to the parents and the same-sex
friend than unmarried Ss, and (b) there was more disclosure to
the Spouse than to any other target-person by married or unmarried Ss.

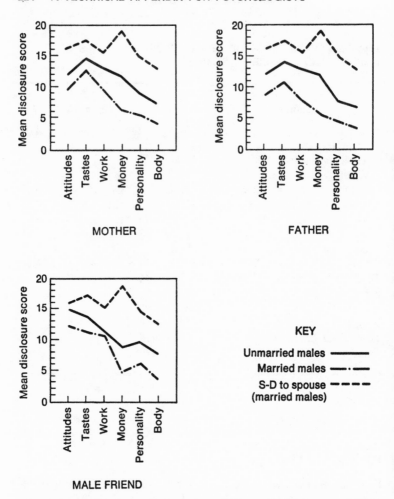

Figure 2 Comparison of Married and Unmarried Males on Self-Disclosure to Mother, Father, and Male Friend. (The curve for disclosure to Spouse is shown in each panel.)

Marriage thus appears to have the effect, not of increasing or decreasing the total extent to which Ss disclose themselves, but of producing a redistribution of self-disclosure. The married Ss "concentrated" self-disclosure upon the spouse, and became more reticent toward other persons. In this sense, self-disclosure enters into relations similar to those of libido in psychoanalytic theory.

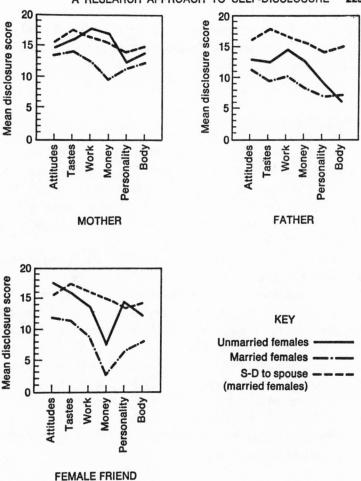

Figure 3 Comparison of Married and Unmarried Females on Self-Disclosure to Mother, Father, and Female Friend. (The curve for disclosure to Spouse is shown in each panel.)

Parent-Cathexis and Self-Disclosure to Parents

Total Mother-Cathexis scores for the group of 31 nursing students correlated —.63 with scores for self-disclosure to Mother; Father-Cathexis scores correlated —.53 with scores for self-disclosure to Father. Both coefficients were significant beyond the .01 level for $df = 29$. The direction of the obtained values signifies that high self-disclosure was associated with positive feelings toward the parents, while low self-disclosure was associated with attitudes of dislike toward the parents.

DISCUSSION

These preliminary findings demonstrate that self-disclosure is measurable, and that the present method for assessing it has some validity. The questions now open for exploration are virtually without limit, in view of the many possible and relevant combinations of the main factors—groups, target-persons, aspects of self, and individual differences.

Some questions suggested by the present findings may serve as guides to further exploration: Why do Negro Ss consistently disclose less about themselves than whites, and why do females disclose more than males? Why is the mother the preferred target of self-disclosure for this age group? What is the significance of the fact that some aspects of self, for instance, Tastes and Interests, Attitudes and Opinions, and Work, are disclosed more than information about Personality, Money, and Body? Is it an artifact of the questionnaire, or does it reflect cultural consensus about what is readily disclosable and what is not? What individual traits besides feelings and attitudes toward target-persons account for individual differences in self-disclosure?

SUMMARY

A reliable questionnaire for the assessment of self-disclosure was described. Groups of both sexes, white and Negro, married and unmarried, were tested with the questionnaire for extent of self-disclosure of six different aspects of self to various target-persons—Mother, Father, Male Friend, Female Friend and/or Spouse. The findings are summarized as follows:

1. Young unmarried Ss, both white and Negro, showed the

highest self-disclosure to Mother, with lesser amounts to Father, Male Friend, and Female Friend.

2. Ss tended to vary the amount of self-disclosure with respect to the category of information to which an item about the self belonged. Two clusters of aspects emerged, a high disclosure cluster including Attitudes and Opinions, Tastes and Interests, and Work, and a low disclosure cluster comprised of Money, Personality, and Body.

3. White Ss disclosed more than Negroes, and females more than males.

4. There was significant interaction among groups of Ss, target-persons, and aspects of self.

5. Married Ss disclosed less to Mother, Father, and Same-sex Friend than comparable unmarried Ss. The married Ss disclosed more to their Spouses than to any other target-persons.

6. A significant correlation was found between parent-cathexis and self-disclosure to the parents. The more the parents were liked, the more disclosures were made to them.

A2

Some Findings in the Study of Self-Disclosure (1964)[*]

Whenever one constructs a measuring tool, one wonders whether it is reliable and whether it actually measures what it is supposed to measure. We have been able to demonstrate that our questionnaires (of lengths that include 15, 25, 35, 45, and 60 items) have satisfactory reliability (odd-even coefficients for larger subtotals run in the 80s and 90s), and results until now show this method has some validity. It should not be overlooked, however, that there are always fundamental flaws in any personality measure that is

[*] See my book, *Self-Disclosure: An Experimental Analysis of the Transparent Self* (New York: Wiley, 1971) for a more complete overview of research in this area.

based on self-report. With this precaution in mind, let me proceed to narrate some of our findings.

SUBJECT-MATTER DIFFERENCES

We found that certain categories of personal data are consistently disclosed more fully by our subjects to various target-persons than to others. For example, information bearing upon one's work, one's tastes, hobbies, and interests, one's attitudes toward religion, politics, and the like are evidently more disclosable than the details about one's sex life, one's financial status, and one's feelings and problems in relation to one's body and to one's own personality.[63] There are evidently strong social norms at work here, norms that even extend across the Atlantic, for we found[60] that female college students in England show patterns of disclosure and concealment of subject matter that are almost identical with those found among American coeds. Melikian[83] at Beirut, Lebanon, has shown similarly consistent patterns in Near Eastern samples. Male and female Puerto Rican college students likewise resemble Americans in their differential disclosure of subject matter.[61]

Anyone who has conducted psychotherapy knows that patients will more readily disclose some kinds of personal data and will block, or show resistance, with respect to others. Such resistance has been demonstrated with polygraphic measures taken on patients during therapeutic interviews—for example, Davis and Malmo's[19] work with electromyograms and Dittes' with the GSR.[20] I have shown, by means of what I called my "wiggle-chair" (a stratolounger chair equipped with a movement transducer) that subjects will show increases in their base-rate of movement when they are asked to disclose some kinds of personal data by a given interviewer; and different interviewers elicit different outputs of wiggle, no matter what the subject matter. Of course, there are interactions among interviewee, subject matter and interviewer operative here. Our questionnaire measures also yielded significant interaction between subject matter and target-persons, which signifies only that it makes a difference to whom one discloses what.

TARGET-DIFFERENCES

All our questionnaire studies have shown significant differences in the total amount of personal data that Ss have disclosed to the various target-persons that we included for consideration, viz.: parents, closest friends, and spouse. As you might expect, the spouse is typically the one to whom most is disclosed. Indeed, the amount of mutual disclosure spouses engage in exceeds the amount that unmarried people disclose to anyone, whether parent, relative, or friend.[63] This confirms the view that marriage is the "closest" relationship one can enter, and it may help us the better to understand why some people avoid it like the plague. Anyone who is reluctant to be known by another person and to know another person—sexually and cognitively—will find the prospective intimacy of marriage somewhat terrifying.

Among unmarried subjects, we find a complex pattern of target-preferences that is related to the age of the subjects. Female college students in their late teens indicate that they disclose in about comparable degree to their mothers and closest girl-friends, while they keep their fathers and their present boy-friends somewhat more in the dark. Male college students of similar age keep their parents about equally informed about their subjective being, and in lesser degree, than do females. The person who knows these boys best is their closest male friend. Their female friend is typically disclosed less authentic and varied personal information than is their chum. I must mention the consistency with which we found that the father is disclosed to in the least degree by our subjects. Father is evidently kept more in the dark about the subjective side of his children than are other people. He is the last to know what is going on. This is a finding of interest to sociologists and psychiatrists alike! We may conclude from findings

like these that the role of the target-person vis-à-vis the self is
an important determiner of disclosing oneself to him.

When we focused more directly upon a given target-person in
a fixed social role, such as parent, or friend, we found some further
correlates of the amount of disclosure. The degree of liking for
a target-person was found to correlate substantially with the
amount disclosed to him—but, interestingly enough, more strik-
ingly among women than among men. We found that women
show this correlation between liking and disclosure to mother,
father, and work-associates;[59, 63] among men, the comparable correlations were markedly lower.[62] This finding strongly suggests that
women are more responsive to their own feelings—that is, they
vary their interpersonal behavior in accord with their feelings more
so than men do. Both sexes show a correlation between the degree
to which they know a given target-person and their disclosure to
him. Men, evidently, trust their brains, their cognition of the
other person more than their feelings, as a condition for self-
disclosure.

Related to degree of knowing is another interesting, and I think
fundamentally important, datum: for males and females alike, a
very strong correlate of disclosure output to a given target-person
was the amount of disclosure input from that person. I called this
input-output correlation the dyadic effect[59, 62] and I have proven
in my own practice that it extends to the realm of psychotherapy.
I have suggested further that the capacity to disclose authentically,
in response that is appropriate to the setting, to the authentic disclosure of the other person in a dyad is probably one of the best
indicants of healthy personality. It betokens, to use Buber's[9] terms,
the capacity to enter into and sustain dialogue. I think that overly
technical psychotherapists as well as novices probably fall down on
the ability to give an authentic, self-revealing response to the disclosures of their patients, and block, thereby, the ongoing process
of the therapeutic dialogue. In Buber's terms, they have the
capacity for "distance," but not for "entering into relation."
Probably, they are still painfully self-conscious about their tech-

niques, and the therapeutic dyad for them is a secret triad—the supervisor is psychically more present to the novice than is the patient. Likely, too, they have little faith or trust either in the healing powers of their own real selves or in the good will of their patients who would come to know them.

GROUP-DIFFERENCES

In this context, I will report some of the overall differences between groups that we found with our questionnaire measures. You must keep in mind that we were measuring the amount disclosed by an individual to four target-persons. Since there was always interaction between group and target-person, the possibility exists that total disclosure scores based on the sum for all four target-persons may not be different, and yet there could be significant differences between groups in the amount disclosed to a given target-person. The findings I wish to report now were ones in which the difference is disclosure output was general—that is, it extended across target-persons.

The most consistent difference we found was between the sexes, with women indicating that they disclosed more about themselves than men.[55, 63] I must qualify this finding by saying that it has not been without exception in my studies, and at least two investigators in the northeast failed to find a sex difference at all. Thus, Rickers-Ovsiankina and Kusmin[98] at Connecticut and Zief[132] at Harvard did not find the women to be higher disclosers than the men. In fact, Rickers-Ovsiankina found her college male subjects to be slightly more "socially accessible" than women. It is tempting to suggest that in the southeast, where I collected the bulk of my data, the men are men and the women are women; whereas Harvard males and Radcliffe females, whom Zief tested, for example, may not be so different from one another. More generally, the magnitude of the sex-difference in disclosure-output between different groups may be an illuminating phenomenon to study in its own right. I have some data which show that the size of the sex-difference varies in a non-chance way among groups who differed in their performance on the Minnesota Multiphasic Personality Inventory, for example.

In the realm of national differences, we found[60] that English co-eds were consistently lower disclosures to the significant people in their lives than comparable American females. Melikian[82] did not find differences between nine different Far Eastern samples in *total* disclosure output, but did find a significant group by target interaction. He did not report his target means, a serious oversight, so we do not know on which target persons his various populations differed in disclosure output. However, I compared the mean total disclosure scores he reported with scores obtained by male college students tested with a questionnaire identical with his, and the American mean totals were substantially higher. No test for the significance of the difference was possible.

I have some recent data[61] showing comparisons between N's of 25 male and 25 female Puerto Rican college students with the same N's of American college students, matched for age, religion (mostly Catholic), and fathers' occupational level. The Puerto Ricans had significantly lower total disclosure scores than the Americans. Among the males, the differences extended across all four target persons. In the female sample, the Americans disclosed more to Father, opposite-sex friend, and same-sex, friend, but less to Mother than did the Puerto Rican girls. It may well be true that Americans talk more about themselves to others than just about any other cultural group.

A study of interdenominational differences showed that Catholic, Methodist, and Baptist college males did not differ significantly from one another in disclosure output, but they all disclosed less, on the average, than Jewish male college students. Among the females, these denominations did not differ among one another, suggesting that their sex-role was a stronger determiner of their self-disclosing behavior than their religious affiliation.[56] One wonders at the greater openness of the Jewish males in comparison with their non-Jewish fellow students. Perhaps it betokens a greater need or capacity for intimate personal relationships than is typical for the American culture at large.

I collected data (unpublished) which showed that applicants for clinical services at the campus psychological counseling center were lower disclosers than matched groups of students who had not sought such services. The main trend approached significance, but it tended to be obscured by the fact that some of the applicants for counseling obtained unusually *high* disclosure scores, especially to their parents, in comparison with controls. This suggests that excessive disclosure may be as incompatible with optimum adjustment in the college milieu as unduly low disclosure. Parenthetically, I may add that in one study I cited above,[59] the two women least liked by their colleagues were, respectively, the highest and lowest disclosures of self in their work setting.

Here is a finding that may interest those who are concerned with gerontology. We found[49] that, as people get older, the amount they disclose to other people in their lives, especially parents and same-sex friend, gradually diminishes. Disclosure to opposite-sex friend, or spouse, increases from the age of 17 up to about the fifties and then drops off. It is possible that, with increased age, the communicative intimacy of relationships with others diminishes, possibly an illustration of the disengagement phenomenon that Henry and Cummings[40] have written about.

Another group difference that warrants mention has to do with rated interpersonal competence. We tested nursing students with a disclosure questionnaire.[58] A year later, at the end of their period of clinical practice, they were rated for ability to establish and maintain a communicative relationship with patients. The students who received the highest rating were significantly higher disclosers on the test they had taken the year before than the students receiving the lower ratings. It would appear that those who were most accustomed to making their own subjective being accessible to others learned the most readily to elicit the subjective being of others.

Again with nursing students, we found substantial correlations between scores for disclosure to mother and to girl-friend (obtained while the girls were sophomores) and accumulated grade-point average in nursing courses at time of graduation. The students were graded, in nursing courses, not only for knowing correct answers on objective quizzes, but also for ability to convey to their instructors the meaning of their experience at working with patients, reading assorted books and papers, etc., in so-called reaction papers and on essay examinations. Evidently those students least able to be open with female target-persons were least able to behave in the open way with the nursing faculty, the way which seemed to facilitate learning and performance of the valued sort. Two years later, I repeated this study, with a different self-disclosure questionnaire, and got comparable results, though the correlations were not so high.

Here is a group difference which is of a different sort,[94] but one fraught with implications, I believe. Powell tested a group of underachieving college students at the University of Florida with a self-disclose questionnaire and with a test of personal security. We anticipated that the underachievers would be lower disclosers and more insecure people than a matched group of adequately achieving students. There were no differences between these groups in mean disclosure to any target-person, and there was some slight evidence that achieving males (but not females) were more independently secure than underachieving subjects. Then, we turned up a nice nugget. Among the achieving males and females, significant correlations were found between closeness to peers and personal security; the comparable r's among underachievers were not significant. Among underachievers, significant r's were found between disclosure to each parent and personal security. Such was not the case among the achievers. We interpreted these findings to mean that underachieving students were less mature, in the sense of being less emancipated from parents, than were achieving students. In other words, security among the underachievers was a function of the intimacy of the relationship with the parents, while security in the achieving groups was more independent of the vicissitudes of the parent-child relationship. Some further evidence that the correlation between self-disclosure scores and measures of intraindividual traits betoken dependency is provided by some data obtained by Terence Cooke,[18] who did a doctoral dissertation with me. He devised a measure of "manifest religious behavior" for Protestants. This questionnaire gets at the intensity of religious involvement by asking Ss to indicate the frequency with which they attend church, the amount of donation, frequency of prayer, etc. Cooke found insignificant r's between measures of disclosure to parents and strength of manifest religious behavior in a sample of 111 male college students between the ages of 17 and 22. I re-analyzed his data, this time computing separate correlations between disclosure to mother and father and religious behavior for 17-18 year-olds, 19 year-olds, 20 year-olds, and 21-22 year-olds. I found that there were significant r's for the first two age levels, but not for the latter two. This finding indicates that religiosity is related to the degree of closeness to parents among late teen-agers, but becomes more independent of the parent-child relationship as the child becomes older. The utilization of the correlation between an interpersonal measure (self-disclosure scores) and an intrapersonal measure as an indicator of an underlying construct has intriguing methodological implications, it seems to me. It may, for example, point to a dimension of interpersonal "influencability" that is present in one group but not in another. The construct might then be approached more directly by other measurement procedures.

We may conclude from all these data, and my tentative inferences from them, that self-disclosure is a measurable facet of man's being and his behavior, and that understanding of its conditions and correlates will enrich our understanding of man in wellness and in disease.

Possible Points of Departure
for Research in Spirit

1. Collect, by advertisement in medical and nursing journals, critical incidents which describe unusual experiences with placebos and descriptions of well-nigh miraculous recovery from imminent death. Search for common factors.

2. Review literature on studies of morale, of "suggestion," of faith and faith-healing.

3. Study people who live productive, loving lives.

4. Set up experimental hospital wards devoted to probing the limits of healing through mobilization of spirit, to discovering what patients have most faith in. Learn graduated dosages thereof; take regular physiological and biochemical measures to discern effects.

5. Study "inspiring" teachers and physicians and nurses. The

problem of locating these: suggest peer-nominations, and nominations by students and patients.

6. Study psychogenic death.

7. Identify the Joe and Jane "Btflsks" (contemporary witches) in our society, study them and their impact on others, how they go about demoralizing and dispiriting others.

8. Try to localize, even roughly, the brain site of the neurophysiological counterpart of faith, *joie-de-vivre*, enthusiasm, etc.

9. Find a moderately sick patient who has faith in blood transfusion. Connect him to EEG, EMG, EKG, PGR, make blood-samples at minute intervals, tape-record his introspective free-association account—but give *no* transfusion, although he believes life- and health-giving fluids are gradually being infused into a vein. Maybe the correlated data would point to some central locus of faith.

10. Study the habits and commitments of aged people at old-age homes and seek relationships between inspirited commitments and death-age. Set up experimental group of people rated as dispirited and strive to inspirit them; also compare their death rate with a control group.

11. Train nurses more effectively to discover means of inspiriting—e.g., "personalized" *geisha* nursing—and compare recovery rates and other pertinent measures with those taken from impersonally nursed patients.

12. Try, through conditioning, hypnosis, or high-prestige suggestion, to convince a population of the effectiveness of some given drug, odor, ritual, etc. See if it is possible to identify the responses which this "substance" affects. Perhaps pattern analysis of the peripheral effects of the substance may point to the more central loci of faith and the spirit-responses.

Bibliography

1. Alexander, F., *Psychosomatic Medicine.* New York: Norton, 1950.
2. Allport, G., *Becoming.* New Haven: Yale Univ. Press, 1955.
3. Anonymous, "A New Theory of Schizophrenia," *J. abn. soc. Psychol.,* 1958, 57, 226–236.
4. Bakan, D., *Pain, Disease, And Sacrifice. Toward A Psychology Of Suffering.* Chicago: Univ. of Chicago Press, 1968.
5. Barr, S., *Purely Academic.* New York: Simon & Schuster, 1958.
6. Berne, E., *Games People Play.* New York: Grove, 1964.
7. Block, J., "The Assessment of Communication. Role Variations As a Function of Interactional Context," *J. Pers.,* 1952, 21, 272–286.
8. Block, J., and Bennett, Lillian, "The Assessment of Communication. Perception and Transmission As a Function of the Social Situation," *Hum. Relat.,* 1955, 8, 317–325.
9. Buber, M., "Elements of the Interhuman," William Alanson White Memorial Lectures. *Psychiatry,* 1957, 20, 95–129.
10. Buber, M., *I and Thou.* New York: Scribners, 1937.
11. Buber, M., *The Knowledge Of Man.* New York: Harper & Row, 1965.
12. Bugental, J. F. T., *The Search For Authenticity. An Existential-*

Analytic Approach To Psychotherapy. New York: Holt, Rinehart & Winston, 1965.

13. Cameron, N. and Magaret, Ann, *Behavior Pathology.* Boston: Houghton Mifflin, 1951.
14. Cannon, W. B., (Voodoo death—chapter on suicide)
15. Canter, A., "The Efficacy of a Short Form of the MMPI to Evaluate Depression and Morale Loss," *J. consult. Psychol.,* 1960, *24,* 14–17.
16. Christenson, W. N., Kane, F. D., Wolff, H. G., and Hinkle, L. E. Jr., "Studies in Human Ecology: Perceptions of Life Experiences As a Determinant of the Occurrence of Illness," *Clin. Res.,* 1958, *6,* 238.
17. Combs, A., and Snygg, D. *Individual Behavior.* (2nd. ed.), New York: Harper, 1959.
18. Cooke, T. F., "Interpersonal Correlates of Religious Behavior," unpublished Ph.D Dissertation, Univ. of Florida, 1962.
19. Davis, F. H., and Malmo, R. B., "Electromyographic Recording During Interview," *Amer. J. Psychiat.,* 1951, *107,* 908–916.
20. Dittes, J. E., "Extinction During Psychotherapy of GSR Accompanying 'Embarrassing' Statements," *J. abn. soc. Psychol.,* 1957, *54,* 187–191.
21. Dunn, H. L., "High-level Wellness for Man and Society," *Amer. J. Pub. Health,* 1959 (b), *49,* 786–792.
22. Durkheim, E., *Suicide.* Glencoe: Free Press, 1951.
23. Engel, G. L., "Studies of Ulcerative Colitis, V. Psychological Aspects and Their Implications for Treatment." *Amer. J. Digest. Dis.,* 1958, *3,* 315–337.
24. Eysenck, H. J., "The Effects of Psychotherapy: an Evaluation," *J. consult. Psychol.,* 1952, *16,* 319–324.
25. Fiedler, F. E., "A Comparison of Therapeutic Relationships in Psychoanalytic Non-directive, and Adlerian Therapy," *J. consult. Psychol.,* 1950, *14,* 436–445.
26. Fiedler, F. E., "A Note on Leadership Theory: The Effect of Social Barriers between Leaders and Followers," *Sociometry,* 1957, *20,* 87–94.
27. Foote, N. N., and Cottrell, L. S. *Identity and Interpersonal Competence.* Chicago: Univ. of Chicago Press, 1955.
28. Frank J. D., *Persuasion and Healing.* Baltimore: Johns Hopkins Univ. Press, 1961.
29. Frankl, V. E., *The Doctor and the Soul, An Introduction to Logotherapy.* New York: Knopf, 1955.
30. Frankl, V. E., *From Death Camp to Existentialism.* Boston: Beacon Press, 1959.

31. Freud, S., *The Interpretation of Dreams*. New York: Basic Books, 1955.
32. Fromm, E., *The Art of Loving*. New York: Harper, 1956.
33. Fromm, E., *Man for Himself*. New York: Rinehart, 1947.
34. Fromm, E., *The Sane Society*. New York: Rinehart, 1955.
35. Gergen, K., "Social Reinforcement of Self-presentation Behavior," unpublished Ph.D. Dissertation, Duke Univ., 1962.
36. Goldstein, K., *Human Nature in the Light of Psychopathology*. Cambridge: Harvard Univ. Press, 1947.
37. Goodman, G. E., "Emotional Self-disclosure in Psychotherapy," unpublished Ph.D. Dissertation, Univ. of Chicago, 1962.
38. Greenspoon, J., "The Reinforcing Effect of Two Spoken Sounds on the Frequency of Two Responses," *Amer. J. Psychol.*, 1955, *68*, 409–416.
39. Heider, F., *The Psychology of Interpersonal Relations*. New York: Wiley, 1958.
40. Henry, W. E., and Cumming, Elaine, "Personality Development in Adulthood and Old Age," *J. proj. Tech.*, 1959, *23*, 383–390.
41. Hinkle, L. E., and Wolff, H. G., "Ecologic Investigations of the Relationship between Illness, Life Experiences and the Social Environment," *Ann. Int. Med.*, 1958, *49*, 1373–1388.
42. Hinkle, L. E., "On the Assessment of the Ability of the Individual to Adapt to His Social Environment and the Relation of This to Health and High-level Wellness," unpublished report presented to subcommittee for the Quantification of Wellness, National Office of Vital Statistics, Washington, D. C., 1959.
43. Hora, T., "The Process of Existential Psychotherapy," *Psychiat. Quart*, 1960, *34*, 495–504.
44. Horney, K., *Neurosis and Human Growth*. New York: Norton, 1950.
45. Horney, K., *The Neurotic Personality of Our Time*. New York: Norton, 1936.
46. Husserl, E., *Ideas: General Introduction to Pure Phenomenology*. London: Allen and Unwin, 1931.
47. Huxley, A., *Brave New World*. Garden City, New York: Sun Dial Press, 1932.
48. Jahoda, Marie, *Current Concepts of Positive Mental Health*. New York: Basic Books, 1958.
49. Jourard, S. M., "Age and Self-disclosure," *Merrill-Palmer Quart. Beh. Dev.*, 1961, *7*, 191–197.
50. Jourard, S. M., *Disclosing Man to Himself*. Princeton: Van Nostrand, 1968.

51. Jourard, S. M., "The Effects of Experimenters' Self-disclosure on Subjects' Behavior," in Spielberger, C. (ed.), *Current Topics in Clinical and Community Psychology.* New York: Academic Press, 1969, 109–150.

52. Jourard, S. M., "Ego Strength and the Recall of Tasks," *J. abnorm. soc. Psychol.* 1954, 49, 51–58.

53. Jourard, S. M., "Identification, Parent-cathexis, and Self-esteem," *J. consult. Psychol.*, 1957, 21, 375.

54. Jourard, S. M., "Moral Indignation: A Correlate of Denied Dislike of Parents' Traits," *J. consult. Psychol.*, 1954, 18, 59–60.

55. Jourard, S. M., *Personal Adjustment. An Approach through the Study of Healthy Personality.* New York: Macmillan, 1958 (2nd ed., 1963).

56. Jourard, S. M., "Religious Denomination and Self-disclosure," *Psychol. Rep.*, 1961, 8, 446.

57. Jourard, S. M., *Self-disclosure: An Experimental Analysis of the Transparent Self.* New York: Wiley, 1971.

58. Jourard, S. M., "Self-disclosure and Grades in Nursing College," *J. appl. Psychol.*, 1961, 45.

59. Jourard, S. M., "Self-disclosure and Other Cathexis, 244–47. *J. abn. soc. Psychol.*, 1959, 59, 428–431.

60. Jourard, S. M., "Self-disclosure Patterns in British and American College Females," *J. soc. Psychol.*, 1961, 54, 315–320.

61. Jourard, S. M., "Self-disclosure in the United States and Puerto Rico," unpublished data, 1963.

62. Jourard, S. M., and Landsman, M. J., "Cognition, Cathexis, and the 'Dyadic Effect' in Men's Self-disclosing Behavior," *Merrill-Palmer Quart. Behav. Dev.*, 1960, 6, 178–186.

63. Jourard, S. M., and Lasakow, P., "Some Factors in Self-disclosure," *J. abn. soc. Psychol.*, 1958, 56, 91–98.

64. Jourard, S. M., and Richman, P., "Disclosure Output and Input in College Students," *Merrill-Palmer Quart. Beh. Dev.*, 1963, 9, 141–148.

65. Jourard, S. M., and Secord, P. F., "Body-cathexis and Personality," *Brit. J. Psychol.*, 1955, 46, 130–138.

66. Jung, C. G., *Modern Man in Search of a Soul.* New York: Harcourt Brace (Harvest Books), 1933.

67. Kesey, K., *One Flew over the Cuckoo's Nest.* New York: Signet, 1963.

68. Krasner, L., "Studies of the Conditioning of Verbal Behavior," *Psychol. Bull.*, 1958, 55, 148–170.

69. Leary, R., *Interpersonal Diagnosis of Personality.* New York: Ronald, 1957.

70. Laing, R. D., *The Divided Self.* London: Pelican Books, 195.
71. Laing, R. D., *The Politics of Experience and The Bird of Paradise.* London: Penguin, 1967.
72. Laing, R. D., *The Self and Others.* Chicago: Quadrangle, 1962.
73. Laing, R. D., and Esterson, A. *Sanity, Madness and the Family.* London: Tavistock, 1964.
74. Lewin, K., *A Dynamic Theory of Personality.* New York: McGraw-Hill, 1935.
75. Lewin, K., "Some Social-psychological Differences between the United States and Germany," in Lewin, G. (ed.), *Resolving Social Conflicts: Selected Papers on Group Dynamics, 1935–1946.* New York: Harper, 1948.
76. Lindquist, E. F., *Design and Analysis of Experiments in Psychology and Education.* Boston: Houghton Mifflin, 1953.
77. Luijpen, W., *Existential Phenomenology.* Pittsburgh: Duquesne University Press, 1963.
78. Marcuse, H., *One-dimensional Man.* London: Routledge & Kegan Paul, 1964.
79. Maslow, A. H., *Motivation and Personality.* New York: Harper, 1954.
80. Maslow, A. H., *Toward a Psychology of Being.* Princeton: Van Nostrand, 1961.
81. McLuhan, M., *Understanding Media, Extensions of Man.* New York: McGraw-Hill, 1964.
82. Mechanic, D., and Volkert, E. H., "Stress, illness behavior and the sick role," *Amer. Social Rev.,* 1961, 26, 51–58.
83. Melikian, L., "Self-disclosure among University Students in the Middle East," *J. soc. Psychol.,* 1962, 57, 259–263.
84. Miller, J. G., "Toward a General Theory for the Behavioral Sciences," *Amer. Psychol.,* 1955, 10, 513–531.
85. Moloney, J. C., *The Magic Cloak. A Contribution to the Psychology of Authoritarianism.* Wakefield, Mass.: Montrose Press, 1949.
86. Mowrer, O. H., *The Crisis in Psychiatry and Religion.* Princeton: Van Nostrand, 1961.
87. Murphy, G., *Personality, a Biosocial Approach to Origins and Structure.* New York: Harper, 1947.
88. Orwell, G., *1984.*
89. Parsons, T., "Illness and the Role of the Physician: A Sociological Perspective," *Amer. J. Orthopsychiat.,* 1951, 21, 452–460.
90. Parsons, T., and Bales, R. F., *Family, Socialization, and Interaction Process.* Glencoe: Free Press, 1955.

91. Perls, F., *Gestalt Therapy Verbatim*. Lafayette, Calif.: Real People Press, 1969.
92. Popper, K. R., *The Open Society and Its Enemies*. Princeton: Princeton Univ. Press, 1950.
93. Potter, S., *One-Upmanship; being some account of the activities and teaching of the Lifemanship Correspondence College of Oneupness and Gameslifemastery*. New York: Holt, 1952.
94. Powell, W. J., "Personal Adjustment and Academic Achievement of College Students," unpublished M.A. Thesis, Univ. of Florida, 1962.
95. Reich, W., *Character Analysis*. New York: Orgone Press, 1948.
96. Reik, T., *Listening with the Third Ear*. New York: Harcourt, Brace, 1949.
97. Rickers-Ovsiankina, Maria, "Social Accessibility in Three Age Groups," *Psychol. Reports*, 1956, 2, 283–294.
98. Rickers-Ovsiankina, Maria, and Kusmin, A. A., "Individual Differences in Social Accessibility," *Psychol. Rep.*, 1958, 4, 391–406.
99. Riesman, D., *The Lonely Crowd*. New Haven: Yale Univ. Press, 1950.
100. Roethlisberger, F. J., and Dickson, W. J., *Management and the Worker*. Cambridge: Harvard Univ. Press, 1939.
101. Rogers, C. R., "The Characteristic of a Helping Relationship," *Pers. Guid. J.*, 1958, 37, 6–16.
102. Rogers, C. R., "The Concept of the Fully Functioning Person," in Rogers, C. R., *On Becoming a Person*. Boston: Houghton Mifflin, 1961.
103. Rogers, C. R., *Freedom to Learn*. Columbus, Ohio: Merrill, 1969.
104. Rogers, C. R., "A Theory of Psychotherapy with Schizophrencies and a Proposal for Its Empirical Investigation," in Dawson, J. G., Stone H. K., and Dellis, N. P., *Psychotherapy with Schizophrenics*. Baton Rouge: Univ. of Louisiana Press, 1961.
105. Rogers, C. R., and Dymond, R. F., *Psychotherapy and Personality Change*. Chicago: Univ. of Chicago Press, 1954.
106. Rosenthal, D., and Frank J. D., "Psychotherapy and the Placebo Effect," *Psychol. Bull.*, 1956, 53, 294–302.
107. Ruesch, J., *Disturbed Communication*. New York: Norton, 1957.
108. Satre, J. P., *Being and Nothingness*. London: Methuen, 1956.
109. Sartre, J. P., *No Exit*.
110. Schmale, A. H., "Relation of Separation and Depression to Disease," *Psychosom. Med.*, 1958, 20, 259–277.
111. Shutz, W., *Joy*. New York: Grove, 1967.
112. Selye, H., *The Physiology and Pathology of Exposure to Stress*. Montreal: Acta, 1950.

113. Shapiro, A. K., "A Contribution to a History of the Placebo Effect," *Behav. Sci.*, 1960, 5, 109–135.
114. Shaw, F. J. *Reconciliation, a Theory of Man Transcending* (S. M. Jourard, and D. C. Overlade, eds.). Princeton: Van Nostrand, 1966.
115. Skinner, B. F., *Science and Human Behavior*. New York: Macmillan, 1953.
116. Skinner, B. F., "Teaching Machines," *Science*, 1958, 128, 969–977.
117. Skinner, B. F., *Walden Two*. New York: Macmillan, 1948.
118. Smith, Dorothy M., "A Nurse and a Patient," *Nursing Outlook*, February, 1960.
119. Smith, S., "Self-disclosure Behavior Associated with Two MMPI Code Types," unpublished M. A. Thesis, University of Alabama, 1958.
120. Sorokin, P., "The Mysterious Energy of Love," *Main Currents*, September, 1958. Foundation for Integrated Education, Inc., New York.
121. Spielberger, C. (ed.)., *Current Topics in Clinical and Community Psychology*. New York: Academic Press, 1969.
122. Stahmer, H., *Speak, That I May See Thee*. New York: Macmillan, 1969.
123. Standal, S. W., and Corsini, R. J. (eds.), *Critical Incidents in Psychotherapy*. Englewood Cliffs, N. J.: Prentice-Hall, 1959
124. Strupp, H., and Luborsky, L., *Research in Psychotherapy* (Volume 2). Washington: American Psychological Association, 1962.
125. Szasz, T., *The Myth of Mental Illness*. New York: Hoeber, 1961.
126. Tillich, P., *The Courage to Be*. New Haven: Yale Univ. Press, 1952.
127. Truax, C. B. and Carkhuff, R. R., *Toward Effective Counseling and Psychotherapy: Training and Practice*. Chicago: Aldine, 1967.
128. Van Kaam, A., "Phenomenal Analysis: Exemplified by a Study of the Experience of 'Really Feeling Understood,' " *J. individ. Psychol.*, 1959, 15, 66–72.
129. Webb, E. J., Campbell, D. T., Schwartz, R. D., and Sechrest, L., *Unobtrusive Measures. Nonreactive Research in the Social Sciences*. Chicago: Rand-McNally, 1966.
130. Whitehorn, J. C., "The Goals of Psychotherapy," in Rubinstein, E. A., and Parloff, M. B. (eds.), *Research in Psychotherapy*. Washington, D. C.: American Psychological Association, 1959.
131. Wolff, H. G., *Stress and Disease*. Springfield: C. C. Thomas, 1953.
132. Zief, R. M. "Values and Self-disclosure," unpublished Honors Thesis, Harvard Univ., 1962.

Name Index

Pages cited below include references both to names themselves and to superscript bibliographic citations of works by these authors.

Subject Index